*Selling on the Green*

# Selling on the Green

## The Art of Building Trusted Relationships and Growing Your Business on the Golf Course

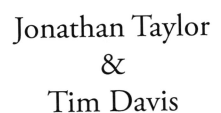

### Jonathan Taylor
### &
### Tim Davis

Selling on the Green
Copyright ©2017 by Jonathan Taylor & Tim Davis
All rights reserved.
Published by Frisco Publishing

No part of this publication may be reproduced, stored in a retrieval system, or transmitted in any form or by any means—electronic, mechanical, photocopy, recording, or any other—without the prior permission of the author.

ISBN-13: 978-154-8311278

Printed in the United States of America

"Trust is the glue of life. It's the most essential ingredient in effective communication. It's the foundational principle that holds all relationships."

- Stephen Covey

# Table of Contents

General Editors ................................................................................................... ix

About Our Contributors ..................................................................................... x

Acknowledgements......................................................................................... xvii

Selling on the Green "Fore"-word by Larry Jackson...................................... xix

Interview with Allen Wronowski, 37th President of the PGA
of America............................................................................................................ 1

Introduction....................................................................................................... 11

Strategic Partnerships on the Golf Course ..................................................... 17
- Jonathan Taylor

Creating Powerful Connections and Staying Top of Mind................................ 21
- Tim Davis

How To Grow Your Business, Build Relationships, and
Help a Charity! ...................................................................................................27
- Joshua Lykins

Golf and Your Personal Brand ......................................................................... 31
- Dr. Deborah M. Gray

Developing the Emotional Bank Account on the Green ................................ 37
- Jonathan Taylor

Advice for Mixing Business with Golf: Don't Do It ......................................... 41
- Bill Johnson

Success on the Golf Course Means Having a Plan ........................................ 47
- Matt Middendorp

How Golf Provides Opportunity for Woman in Business ............................... 53
- Pam Swensen

How Golf Helps Women Gain More Sales through Relationship
Building ............................................................................................................. 59
- Jennifer Harris

Golf: A Game of Integrity, Dignity, and Enjoyment ........................ 63
- Justin Follmer

How to Use the "Little Birdie Strategy" to Let Your Prospects Know You Have the Best Product or Service .............................................. 69
- Rob Wilson

Why the ROI on a Well Planned Round of Golf is Significantly Higher than Most Marketing Tactics Companies Use ...................... 73
- Ken Cook

How One Round of Golf Can Reveal Everything You Need to Know About a Potential Client .............................................................. 81
- Dan Pincus

What's Behind the Pink Tee .......................................................... 85
- Terry Coleman ...........................................................................

The Consequences of "Hard Selling" During Golf ........................ 91
- Scot Duke

How to Create Memorable Experiences on the Golf Course for Your Clients ................................................................................. 99
- Eli Goodrich

Creating Lifelong Friendships and Influential Networks through Golf ............................................................................................ 105
- Cliff Theriault

There Are No Shortcuts to Building Relationships on the Green ... 109
- Tami Belt

A Fuzzy Golf Outing:
How a Well Planned Event Can Make the Difference .................... 115
- Steven Wilson

Protocol and Politeness are Par for the Course ............................... 117
- Dawn Bryan

The Ability to Comeback ............................................................. 125
- Dan Demuth

Why the Mental Game is Crucial to Both Golf and Business ........ 129
- Dr. Dan Schaeffer

Glossary of Golf Terms ................................................................. 139

# General Editors

Tim Davis was an "at-risk" kid from the projects, who learned the valuable lesson of building his network from a young age.

Over his career, he has continued to work on ways to connect with people and share what he has learned with others, so they can build their careers and businesses.

In addition to speaking and consulting, Tim shares his thoughts on branding, marketing, and leadership at TheMarketingEvangelist.com.

Jonathan Taylor is founder of Buzz Mountain Media and the author of four books including his recent bestseller *Launch It: How to Use Videos, Podcasting, Online Media and Viral Marketing to Become a Recognized Expert in Any Industry*. Along with his passion for sales and marketing, Jonathan is an outdoor enthusiast with golf being one of his favorite sports.
You can follow his sales blog and podcast at www.SalesWarriorInc.com.

# About Our Contributors

Tami Belt is the president of Blue Cube Marketing Solutions in Las Vegas, Nevada. Her father was a PGA teaching pro in Las Vegas for more than 40 years, so she grew up on a golf course. A natural storyteller and community catalyzer, Tami Belt was destined to use her creativity and passion for building relationships. She wanted to be a rock star when she grew up, but couldn't sing on key, so she sings the praises of others. You can find out more about her business at 1bluecube.com.

Dawn Bryan is the author of *Elite Etiquette*. Dawn's impressive career includes being selected as a consultant and advisor on international protocol for many luxury brands: Gucci, Neiman Marcus, American Express, Business Week Magazine, Hammacher Schlemmer, Citicorps/Diners Club, Swarovski Crystal, and Waterford Wedgewood, to name a few.

Dawn is the author of the best-selling book, *The Art and Etiquette of Gift Giving* (Bantam), and has authored many articles, columns, and books on the subjects of etiquette, gift-giving, and the quality of things for Business Week, Town & Country, Modern Bride, Vogue, and Glamour, among others.

About Our Contributors | xi

Terry Coleman is a professional realtor from Middle Tennessee. Golf has been an important part of his life and has opened many doors, including many real estate deals. You can find him at tammyandterrycoleman.com.

Ken Cook is the Co-Founder of How To WHO, Inc. and Co-Author of *How to WHO: Selling Personified*, a book and program for building business through relationships. Ken's writing includes: *The Wisdom of Our Peers*; *The AMA Complete Guide to Small Business Marketing*; *The AMA Guide to Strategic Planning for Small Business*; and monthly columns for multiple city business journals.

Ken has spoken at Inc. Magazine Conferences, National Innovation Workshops for The U.S. Chamber of Commerce, and for Fortune 500 companies, including IBM, AT&T, NCR, and Verizon. You can find out more about Ken by visiting howtowho.com.

Dan Demuth, aka "The Golf Whisperer," started his career on the links as a professional golfer, and, now, coaches golfers and business executives alike.

He is the president of Performance in Motion and author of the book: *Secrets of the Golf Whisperer: On & Off the Course.* You can learn more by visiting performanceinmotion.biz.

Scot Duke is CEO of Innovative Business Golf Solutions, LLC. Scot is also known as "Mr. Business Golf." The name came about soon after Scot Duke published the book: *How to Play Business Golf.* During a business networking event, Mr. Duke was surprisingly introduced to the gathering as "Mr. Business Golf." The name stuck, and the rest is history. You can find out more about Scot by visiting mrbusinessgolf.com.

Justin Follmer, MBA, is an independent Investment Advisor Representative with over eight years of experience in the financial services industry. He grew up in the small town of South Williamsport, in north central Pennsylvania, famous as the birthplace of Little League Baseball. During his college years, he enlisted in the United States Marine Corps, where he completed one tour of duty in Iraq during Operation Iraqi Freedom II, with Marine Wing Support Squadron 472 of Wyoming, PA. You can find out more about Justin by visiting lowcountryadvisors.com.

*About Our Contributors* | xiii

Eli Goodrich is President at Game Changer Sales. GCS builds revenue and markets by creating a pipeline and closing sales for start-ups and early stage companies in the USA, as well as internationally. You can learn more at gamechangersales.com.

Jennifer Harris is an entrepreneur, public speaker, ROI Golf Strategist, and founder & CEO of High Heel Golfer, a company dedicated to introducing, instructing, educating, and empowering upwardly mobile, professional women to use golf for business. You can find more about High Heel Golfer at highheelgolfer.com.

Dr. Deborah M. Gray is a Professor of Marketing at Central Michigan University in Mt. Pleasant, Michigan where she teaches marketing strategy and branding in a top-ranked MBA Program. She teaches a business course every spring in Scotland, United Kingdom where CMU students learn the value of building business relationships on the golf course while also learning about golf's deep historical and cultural ties to Scotland. She met and married her husband Trevor at Bucks Run Golf Course.

Joshua Lykins is a business professional who lives in Hermitage, Tennessee. With 16 years' experience as a Golf Professional, he has been directing events and fundraising all over the country for various organizations. He's the founder and president of Elite Events of Music City. You can find out more about Joshua's business at eliteeventsofmusiccity.com.

Matt Middendorp is an award winning trainer, sales manager, speaker, sales mathematician, and owner of Sales Math Consulting LLC. He is the recipient of the 2006 Citizens Bank Grand Rewards prize, 2007 and 2008 member of Associated Bank's President's Club, and, in 2011, was nominated as one of 13 Emerging Leaders in sales. After 18 years of training and leading sales teams, Matt debuted his "Formula for Sales Success" and launched Sales Math Consulting LLC in 2013. You can learn more about Sales Math by visiting sales-math.com.

Dan Pincus has over 25 years of marketing, business development, and management experience. He's built companies and developed relationships with many executives, throughout the NY/NJ metro area. Dan is the president of World Golf Network. You can find out more by visiting worldgolfnetwork.com.

Dan Shaefer, Ph.D., is president of Peak Performance Strategies LLC. He works with people in business, sports & entertainment, and has developed breakthrough strategies in sports performance for professionals: NFL, NHL Goaltenders, Major League Soccer, boxing, ultra & extreme runners, golf, tennis, skiing, and amateur athletes. Consultants, sports agents, GMs, and coaches also rely on Dr. Dan to get their teams performing at their best. You can learn more about Dr. Dan by visiting danschaeferphd.com.

Pam Swensen is CEO of the executive Women's Golf Association (EWGA), an organization dedicated to enriching the lives of women, through the game of golf. With 25 years of developing relationships and connections within the golf industry, Pam has received many industry honors for growing the game of golf, opening doors to women, and being a top women-lead business CEO. You can find more about the Woman's Golf Association at ewga.com.

Bill Johnson is a golf fanatic and veteran sales professional with over 30 years' experience. He's the president and CEO of Salesvue, a software solution that brings automation and insight to the outbound sales process. You can find out more about his company at salesvue.com

Rob Wilson is a financial adviser who works with a number of professional athletes and executives. Additionally, Rob hosts a podcast called "Movers and Shakers," where he interviews people about their unique business strategies. You can find out more about Rob by visiting RobWilson.tv.

Cliff Theriault is a Regional Manager for CMG Financial, a privately held mortgage-banking firm, headquartered in San Ramon, CA. He's been involved in the building and managing of Mortgage Companies, throughout his career. He's a former President of the Illinois Mortgage Bankers. Cliff has coached football and baseball for over 30 years and enjoys playing golf as often as he can. He's been married for 43 years to his wife, Lela.

Steven Wilson is president of SMW Marketing Works. He has a distinguished career in helping executives use golf as a business development tool. His experience has been felt in many areas from corporate outings for Fortune 100 companies and the World Amateur Handicap Championship in Myrtle Beach, SC, now the World's largest golf tournament, which he created while at Golf Digest, to the New York Islanders charity golf outing, which he started near his hometown on Long Island, NY. You can learn more about Steven by visiting smwmarketingny.com.

# Acknowledgements

Thank you to all of our contributing authors: Joshua Lykins, Terry Coleman, Bill Johnson, Dawn Bryan, Dan Demuth, Dan Pincus, Cliff Theriault, Eli Goodrich, Dr. Dan Shaefer, Jennifer Harris, Pam Swensen, Justin Follmer, Matt Middendorp, Rob Wilson, Ken Cook, Steven Wilson, Scot Duke, and Tami Belt.

Thanks to Allen Wronowski, 37th president of the PGA of America for sharing about the wonderful work they're doing with the Folds of Honor.

The stories and the lessons they represented made this book possible.

Finally, a big thank you to Larry Jackson for agreeing, on short notice, to write the foreword for this book.

*Jonathan Taylor*

*Tim Davis*

# Selling on the Green
# "Fore"-word by Larry Jackson

Golf has been a significant part of my business strategy for 25 years. In the beginning, I didn't realize I was being strategic (which means I wasn't); I was just playing golf with whomever would play with me. But, as years went by, it became apparent how golf can help form lasting business relationships and friendships.

During my childhood, golf played second fiddle to baseball, basketball, and soccer. But I did get to golf a couple of times per year with my Dad and his buddies. Those early golf outings, as a nine-year-old, served me well, regarding the rules of golf, etiquette, fast play, walking and carrying, and the esoteric, yet omnipresent, art of the golf "betting game."

"Hey, Kid," my Dad's buddy said, "we're playin' a nassau for dimes, two down auto-presses; I'll give ya five shots a side; your dad has yer first buck: 10 dimes on the house! You're on your own after that."
"And I get to play from the ladies' tees, right?" I said.
"Always lookin' for an angle, arentcha, kid..."

My first job out of college was a gig, teaching golf at a couple of Club

Meds. It sounds like a fake job that exists only in Rick Reilly articles, and I was a very average golfer to boot.

Nonetheless, teaching golf at a Club Med is like being a cruise director - make sure the VIPs understand the course, have fun, and imbibe copious amounts of "vacation juice." Never underestimate the power and influence of "juice" on the golf course, but that's a subject for the foreword of a future book, *Golf and Beer – The Perfect Pairing*.

The true business value of golf became evident to me during the '90s, while living in Asia and working for high-tech telecom equipment manufacturers.

Asia, with its deep-rooted ancient culture mingled with precise business practices, was a fascinating, yet confusing, place for an American businessman that required deep research and sensitivity…and, as it turned out, golf.

Fortunately, business people in Asia are golf crazy and devote an entire day to a round of golf. Spending an uninterrupted, full day with a customer or business partner proved to be a powerful method of strengthening relationships and landing deals. Golf was the universal language, no matter how you slice it.

Golf plays an even bigger business role in my current venture, Loudmouth Golf. It was started in 2000 by my business partner Woody, who designed a few wild golf pants, made a website, and fulfilled the orders right out of his garage.

Woody and I have gravitated towards bright clothing all our lives, and our paths crossed in 2006 when Woody, a burdened and scattered entrepreneur, and I, a disgruntled customer, engaged in a round of golf and delightful banter to discuss the Loudmouth business.

On the front 9 we discussed the problems, on the back 9 we discussed potential solutions, and in the 19th hole we came up with the outline of a partnership.

The game of golf has been growing for generations, but, at the moment, this glorious game of ours is at a crossroads.

*Selling on the Green* explains the many ways that business needs golf and, at the moment, golf needs business. Jonathan & Tim innately understand business and the art of business golf; this book is a pleasure to read, along with being invaluable to the business professional.

Golf with Dad taught me how to bet.

Golf at Club Med taught me how to golf with my elders (and hammerheads).

Golf in High Tech taught me the art of the Big Deal.

Golf with Woody wearing Loudmouth is a real kick in the pants …

Larry Jackson, CEO LoudMouth Golf

Larry Jackson has over 20 years of experience in the Silicon Valley based telecommunications and networking equipment field, in a variety of Sales & Marketing roles.

During his time in the telecom equipment field, he helped found three startup companies, all of which went public on NASDAQ.

Larry has lived and worked internationally, in Tokyo and London, while working for companies experiencing exponential sales growth and expansion, and sees Loudmouth doing the same.

Larry has golfed for business and pleasure around the world. An active investor in LoudMouth since January of 2007, he took on the role of full time CEO in 2008. He claims he's the best golfer on the LMG team.

"Visit Loudmouthgolf.com and get 10% off any merchandise when you use the discount code OnTheGreen10 at checkout."

# Interview with
# Allen Wronowski,
## 37th President of the PGA of America

**Tim Davis:** Listen, I am super excited. We have as our guest Allen Wronowski. Allen was the 37th president of the PGA of American among a countless other accolades and awards and honors. Allen, thanks so much for joining us. Tell us a little bit about your journey of how you got to the level of president of the PGA of America.

**Allen Wronowski:** It's amazing what destiny can bring us to. I was very fortunate to have a career started at a public facility down in southeast Baltimore, Rocky Point Golf Course. And fortunately my head professional was an individual that worked for Bill Clarke, one of our past presidents of the PGA of America at Hillendale Country Club in 1979. He was looking for an assistant professional and out of 83 applicants I got that job. I never realized that I would spend the next 34 years of my life at Hillendale. I went from assistant professional to head professional to director of golf. I met my wife who was my shop manager first. We got married and raised two wonderful children there.

My stepson now actually works in the golf business as well. He's a PGA member and works at the Oakridge Club about 40 minutes away from me. So golf certainly gave me an amazing path for a career and a lifestyle. The members at Hillendale were just incredible. Mr. Clarke was very persuasive in the need to work and try to help other members of the association and to be involved.

So in 1983 he had me start on the assistance committee for the Mid-atlantic Section PGA and from there I went to being a Board member, and I served on numerous committees at the section level. I wound up being elected to section office in 1995. We had a nice little race, an election, and out of three individuals I was elected to serve on the National Board of Directors in 2000. I served in that role for four years and then ran for national election to become secretary of the PGA of America. I was unsuccessful in my first pursuit, which is not uncommon for most of our past presidents.

It's a challenging process when you're trying to convince 27,000 people that you could be the person to give the baton to. So but it was an historic seven ballot election that I lost. Then in 2006 when I ran a second time, I won in three ballots and served the association for two years as secretary to the vice president and two as president.

And now in my final two years as the honorary president of the PGA along with that, I've been on the rules committee for the Masters for years. I've served on the PGA Tour Policy Board. I chaired the Junior PGA Championship six times and will be co-captain of our Junior Ryder Cup Team this year in Scotland at Blairgowrie. As you can see, not a lot of grass growing under my feet.

**Tim Davis:** What's one of your most favorite stories from the time with the PGA?

**Allen Wronowski:** It was interesting that when we did the Ryder Cup, and we were the host country, I was the host president who was standing at a podium in front of 40,000 people and being broadcast to half a billion households. It was a little intimidating. They told us prior to that that airplanes wouldn't be flying overhead from O'Hare and the band wouldn't be jumping up in front of the teleprompter.

Well unfortunately that evening the band was moving around like crazy and swapping music and getting drinks and planes were going overhead like crazy.

So being at that podium and having that little bailiwick was one of the things that my wife was very impressed with - that I kept my composure and it came out real smooth.

I'd say one of the most emotional moments was when we got to do a ceremony at the Tomb of the Unknown Soldier in Arlington. We all walked down with the sergeant of arms. When you overlook those 300,000 plus grave sites, and they begin to play taps and you think of all the amazing military people that have protected our freedoms over the years and have served our country, it gets to be a pretty emotional moment.

**Tim Davis:** That really parlays into Folds of Honor. Can you tell us a little bit about that project and what's happening with that?

**Allen Wronowski:** I certainly can. I served on the Board for the Folds of Honor as an officer of the PGA of America and I was actually secretary of the PGA to President Brian Whitcomb when Major Dan Rooney came to us and wanted to look at pursuing an endeavor, a joint endeavor.

Major Dan Rooney is an F16 pilot who has done three tours of duty in Iraq and he's also a PGA professional in Oklahoma. Major Dan was flying home to see his parents in Michigan, delayed flights and all and getting in really late. And when he came on the plane he saw an individual in dress uniform. The pilot came on when they landed and he asked everyone to remain seated as they were bringing home the remains of Corporal Brock Bucklin who had been killed in action in Iraq.

His twin brother had traveled 7,000 miles to bring the body home. Dan looked out the window and he saw Brock's wife and his three-year-old son Jacob, and he realized at that point there was a need and a mission that he wanted to serve and that was to support and help the families of our heroes who had either been killed or severely disabled in the line of combat.

It's amazing how little support they get from the government and unfortunately nine out of ten families roughly get little to no government assistance at this point. Dan began the Folds of Honor Foundation and over the seven years probably the biggest event that we've run and that we're most known for is Patriot Golf Day. That happens at many facilities on Labor Day weekend. The monies go to support the children and spouses of our heroes that have been killed and severely disabled.

To date, there were 7,000 scholarships given 40 million dollars raised. But the need is just so great and it's growing. It could be up to 700,000 people that could be affected before all is said and done.

This spring we had 3,600 applicants. It's the first time that we actually won't be able to take care of all the needs. From that we've also had Patriot Bowling Days, Patriot Fishing Days through the courtesy of Bass. We've had Patriot Boating Month that began at Liberty Harbor in New York. Suntex and Miramax were great partners. We've had other great companies join us with Budweiser, Jimmy John's, Outback, and the list goes on and on.

To anybody listening I really ask and encourage you please go to our website, www.Foldsofhonor.org.

I would also ask that you go to Facebook if you're on it and certainly like our page. It helps us with the number of followers it has. And follow us on Twitter. You can see all the different events that we're hosting and that we're having.

After 40 years in the golf business I was very, very fortunate to have the experiences I did. Certainly honored to serve the PGA of America in the roles that I did. And you just get to a point if I want to do more and I want to really affect change in the world and make a difference to people.

When Dan talked about an ambassador program to get more localized, regional and to get bigger exposure and to raise awareness about what the Folds of Honor is about and to help generate funds, I said "would you consider me?". He said tell me when you want to start.

So I went to work for them this past March, and each and every day that I get up it's a blessing to try to figure out how we can do more and really help these families. Each and every time we listen to the stories from the scholarship recipients, it's moving. We just had a lady come in with her three-year-old son in our Board meeting at the PGA Championship and she was talking about how she was pregnant with her son Landon and due in about seven months.

Her husband had been deployed just prior to that to Afghanistan and unfortunately all of his body was not protected by Kevlar. The parts that were protected deflected three bullets; but one bullet severed his spinal column in the back of his neck.

She was too far along in her pregnancy to go to Germany to see him on life support and they certainly couldn't bring him back over. When you hear her talk about how important the Folds of Honor was to her - to be able help her go back to school and find a career to raise their son Landon. It meant so much to her, that we were really thinking about the sacrifices that they make. Very simply, the mission of the Folds of Honor is to honor their sacrifice by educating their legacy.

When you see how this is going to impact their lives, it is worth it. Sarah White's story is another compelling example. Her father was a pilot that was killed, and the scholarship helped her complete her education at Auburn. The stories go on and on and on. There's not enough Kleenex.

**Jonathan Taylor:** What a powerful story. What you are doing at the Folds is such a fantastic cause.

**Allen Wronowski:** And there's just so many ways for people that are listening to this to get involved whether you want to volunteer at a facility that's running an event. If you can make a donation; if you participate in one of the Patriot events, that's fabulous. And again just really helping us out by liking us and following us on the Twitters and Facebooks. There's some neat products that you'll find that are out there with Folds of Honor logo on them that you can purchase and the proceeds of those go to Folds. There's just a lot of ways to get involved.

**Jonathan Taylor:** What is your impression of the game currently compared to past years, and what are your thoughts on the level of commitment and interest today?

**Allen Wronowski:** There are people that think the glass is half full, people that think it's half empty and I personally think it's a trick question. I think the glass is always full of something. It's either air or liquid. It's not in a vacuum. It's got to have something in it.

**Allen Wronowski:** So certainly starting in the seventies to today I've seen highs and lows. I've seen different scenarios happen and really it's amazing how many people just want to start crying crisis that the game is just in terrible shape.

If you think about the game going from an all-time high of 30 million to roughly 26 million now; that's a pretty small shakeout. Certainly it is a little disconcerting but there's too many of the partners in the industry right now with a focus on trying to make sure that the game thrives. And I think we went through a time period where certainly when you look at our all-time high the game changed a little bit.

In my mind there were too many golf courses built that were too hard. They were too stretched out to sell real estate and we got away from the emphasis. When you go to Europe there's not a lot of property involved. They just do it with the lay of the land.

I always kid and say "why do you think we can't get people to play more?". It's because the golf course is 7,400 yards, it's got a 15 yard wide fairway, a six inch rough, a bunker that's 50 feet high, greens speeds are 16.

It takes you five and a half hours to play and $250. Why wouldn't I want to bring my whole family out for this experience? So what's really good is the superintendents, the architects, a lot of the people in the industry realize that it just got a little out of hand.

We've seen people now with multiple sets of tees. When I first went to Hillendale we had three sets of tees. And now we have seven sets between the U.S. kids at 2,000 and 3,000 all the way to our back tees and then a combination of different other tee pads can be used.

We've got to get people thinking of playing the game at a level that's fun; kind of like the tour players. Barney Adams was very instrumental with the Tee It Forward in helping us move that needle saying look, so if the best players are getting a seven iron to a par four, what yardage do you need to play where you can reach a par four with a seven iron or an eight iron like they do. What yardage do you need to play where you can have a reachable par five. We you're hitting middle to short irons to par three. If I make my tee ball about 200 yards and it's more fun. My wife when she plays at a 4,500 yard golf course has a great time. She can reach a lot of greens and has some fun and make some birdies.

Being more cognizant I think all of us are aware of the time constraints that people face. And it was interesting when we hired the Boston consulting group to really give us a perspective from the consumer's viewpoint versus more of an internal look, the biggest factor was time. It wasn't money. And the reality is the average green fee in the country was $28 for 18 holes. So there's a lot of affordable golf.

We found it was time, and when people thought about golf they thought about it being a whole day process. Well we don't have to think about golf as 18 holes. Golf can be ten holes. It can be 12 holes. It can be nine holes. It can be six holes. Some facilities are just charging by time. Kind of like bowling. It went from frames to time and if you go out and play for an hour and 15 minutes this is the charge. And you almost get a punch card when you come in to see how long you were out and you're charged on that basis. So that's a good way to do it.

Certainly the impact of our junior program has really gotten very good use. We changed the PGA Sports Academy so it had different levels and it had a lot of different components in there that were fun and really good values of nutrition and certainly the life lessons are now.

Three years ago we started the junior league. Bob Longmire at LEJ Sports came to us and talked about junior league golf. We said we think this will work but it's kind of out there. The kids are ages seven to 13. They get jerseys. You're allowed substitutions. They play three, three-hole formats with nine holes.

The parents and a lot of guardians and grandparents are encouraged to come out and cheer and yell for the kids. It was a pilot program three years ago. It started with about 1,700 kids. Last year we got to about 8,000 kids. This year we'll have about 20,000 kids and the prediction is in the next two years we'll be up to 100,000 kids. And they are really enjoying the game. They're getting their parents out there. They want to play more. It's exciting, it's fun and it's fast form and that's a great thing. When you think about it – we missed a generation really promoting them to play because things looked really good economically. Right now it's getting a better exposure.

**Jonathan Taylor:** That's exciting for the future. I've got an eight year old who's taken up an interest.

**Allen Wronowski:** So I don't forget, let me plug "Get Golf Ready". This is a program under my term. Then vice president Ted Bishop really took the bull by the horns and ran with it. Get Golf Ready is an incredible program for those that have not played or played very limited that's five one-and-a-half hour sessions. Usually it starts at $99. It might be a little bit more depending on areas.

Five one-and-a-half hour sessions with groups of eight or less. And there's the short game, the long game, different specialty shots and there's an on course experience to it. We've seen that the people that have taken these classes, 83 percent of them stay in the game through years two and three. You can find that online at www.GetGolfReady.com.

People don't realize how important the game of golf is. If you look at it personally, you realize the health benefits of the game. If you walk 18 holes you burn 2,500 calories roughly and if you ride in the cart for 18 holes you burn 1,500 calories. There's some great health and wellness to it. Being in the open green space environment and the amount of stress reduction is phenomenal. There was as study done in Europe that found golfers tend to live five years longer than non-golfers.

Also, it doesn't matter what you shoot. The other thing people don't realize is how important the game is in the country. I'm very active with the "We Are Golf" initiative. Every year on Capitol Hill, we go tell our legislature about how important the game is.

A lot of people don't know that there are two million jobs associated with the game of golf in this country, with over 50 billion dollars in waged income. And the overall golf industry, direct and indirect, is a 176 billion dollar industry. So the economic impact is really important.

When you look at the charitable aspect of the game, you'll find that each and every year through 140,000 plus events, golf raises 3.9 billion dollars! More than all the other sports combined

You think about the relationships and the friendships that you've made, whether it's with a family member, your neighbors, friends that you get to play with all the time. Even a lot of times people that you just get paired up with. Those relationships and friendships just go forever and they're so solid and tremendous. Great opportunities.

You have the greatest opportunity again for the health and wellness aspect, for the camaraderie aspect. You can use it in business to entertain. You can use it for the social aspect of the game. You can use it to network in your area. You can use it for fundraising. The opportunities just go on and on and on. So great opportunities and lifetime friendships.

**Tim Davis:** Well this has been fantastic! It's been a pleasure and a real honor to have you on with us tonight, Allen.

**Allen Wronowski:** Thank you for giving me the opportunity to talk about something really near and dear to my heart with the Folds of Honor. Please check out www.Foldsofhonor.org. Check out the Facebook and Twitter pages. Feel free to follow and Tweet me.

Feel free to email me at awronowski@foldsofhonor.org. Thanks for all you're doing promoting the game of golf and letting me speak about the PGA of America and the game initiatives as well.

The game to me is in good shape, and I think you're gonna see incredible growth again as we move into the next years.

# Introduction

We all sell. No matter what industry you are in, selling is a part of doing business. Some of us sell products and services, while others sell ideas to people within their organization.

In today's world, your ability to sell an idea, product, or service relies on relationships, not smooth techniques.

Many sales books and coaching programs still seem to focus on the techniques or methods for growing new business.

For example, the majority of today's consultative sales training programs revolve around "problem solving" – identifying your prospect's biggest concerns and showing how your product or service is the solution. While this method is sometimes effective, it only lasts until someone else provides an even better solution.

In our years as sales professionals, and consulting with others, we've seen many lost business opportunities that had very little to do with the value of the product or service and even less to do with the cost.

Instead, it had everything to do with the how well the decision maker liked the other guy.

In many cases, decision makers would choose to spend quite a bit more money to do business with individuals with whom they had a previous relationship.

In his book, Likeability Factor, Tim Sanders identifies four areas of like-ability:

1. *Friendliness* - your ability to communicate a friendly attitude to others.

2. *Relevance* - the ability to connect with another person's wants or needs.

3. *Empathy* - your ability to recognize, acknowledge, and experience other people's feelings.

4. *Realness or authenticity* - the ability to be open and authentic, yet professional, in a business environment.

To sum it up, people buy from those who they know, like, and trust. They buy from people with whom they have a common bond.

We believe the game of golf offers one of the greatest opportunities for building long term relationships, based on these factors.

## *Why Golf is Such an Effective Way to Build Likability and Trust*

In an age when people define relationships by the number of friends on Facebook, and professional connections on LinkedIn, there's something truly special about taking the time to connect with the key individuals who matter in your industry.

This is not a book about improving your golf game, although there are some chapters from contributing authors that offer great tips, for improving your performance.

Instead, we demonstrate through the stories shared, how even an average golfer, if they at least understand the rules and etiquette of the game can use the game to grow trusted business relationships.

You'll find lessons and examples from contributors who have used golf to help grow their businesses. There are stories that show the right way—and the wrong way—to conduct business.

What better way is there for building long-term relationships and determining if there's is a mutual benefit in doing business than spending four hours with someone on the golf course?

In what other networking environment can you learn more about a person's personality, their interests, or their needs?

A thirty-minute sales appointment doesn't offer that. A one-hour business luncheon doesn't offer that. Not even a two-hour social event.

The game of golf offers one of the best settings – a relaxed and fun environment, away from the office, with plenty of time to really learn about the other person.

One common theme among the stories and examples shared in the following chapters is that sales are rarely made during one game.

Originally, the subtitle of this book was: "The Art of Developing Trusted Relationships and Closing More Sales on the Golf Course."

We decided to scratch the word "closing" from the title. That word often has the connotation of a quick, "win at all costs" type of selling.

When people talk of closing, it's easy to picture Alec Baldwin in the movie Glengarry Glen Ross shouting "ABC! Always be Closing!"

Instead we went with the word "growing" and the phrase was changed instead to "Growing Your Business on The Golf Course," because that's what relationship selling is about - growing. It takes time to get to know someone.

It takes time to build those trusted relationships. That can sometimes be difficult in a fast-paced age, where "becoming a friend" happens at the click of a mouse.

The *Selling on the Green* process we've identified for growing long term relationships can be summarized in the graphic below:

Invitation: It all starts with getting your prospect to even accept your invitation to play. This is not always easy with busy professionals, even if they love golf; people can sense when they're getting an invite to a "sales pitch."

In the following chapters, we'll share stories and advice for getting prospects to respond to your invite.

Relationship Building: Your first game is all about getting to know the person you want to do business with. That means it's not a good time to make a proposal. After all, you probably didn't propose to your spouse on the first date. One exception might be if the prospect brings up the topic.

Relationship Management: This is where many sales professionals and entrepreneurs fail. To grow relationships, you have to follow up. That means staying in touch with them after the first game. It's as simple as sending a "thank you" card after the first game, and following up with them regularly afterward.

Most relationships opportunities are lost from a simple lack of follow up.

Uncovering Opportunities: As you manage the relationship, through follow ups and additional opportunities on the golf course, your prospect will be more willing to share their own problems and the vulnerabilities within their organization. These are tremendous opportunities that would never present themselves over a 30 minute meeting or a one hour lunch.

Gaining the Sale: Again, instead of "closing" the sale, we'll use the word gaining, because that's really how it happens. Along with gaining a valuable relationship, you also gain the added benefits of it – the long term sales.

We hope you enjoy the stories and lessons shared in this book.

Some business professionals may look at golf as nothing more than a waste of time and money, but there is a real beauty in the game as a business tool that's often overlooked.

It's one of the few activities that give you the opportunity to spend a half a day really getting to know the other person, with few distractions outside of the occasional beverage cart.

# Strategic Partnerships on the Golf Course

■ Jonathan Taylor

There's nothing quite like spending a weekday afternoon soaking in the sun and enjoying a game of golf, while so many others are stuck behind a desk. But contrary to how that may sound, golf is not all play.

Sometimes you can get more business done in 18 holes than a day of phone calls, e-mails, and lunch appointments. But you have to be strategic about it.

One of the regrets I have, however, is not developing an interest in the game earlier in life.

I played occasionally, when I was in high school and college, with my older brothers, but I didn't really didn't get into golf until after college, when I was working as a manufacturing sales representative, many years ago.

I realized playing golf was an important part of building relationships within my industry. I would get invited to play in tournaments that some of my key customers would host every year, so it was important that I improve not only my skill level, but my understanding of the game.

One of the most effective strategies I found for growing my business with golf was "strategic partnering."

This is a lesson I learned years ago, from legendary, direct-response marketer Jay Abraham, through his book, *Getting Everything You Can Out of All You've Got*.

In his book, he refers to this concept as "host beneficiary relationships," and it simply involves developing strong bonded relationships with other companies that already do business with your prime prospects.

So, instead of inviting my target prospects to play golf, I developed relationships with people who already had a relationship with those prospects.

One of those relationships was with a manufacturing consultant, Steve Campbell, an avid golfer, who worked with some of the same manufacturers I wanted to do business with.

When I was traveling near his area on business, I would call him up and invite him out to play 18 holes. We always had a great time discussing not only golf, but other sports as well.

What you may find interesting is that we rarely discussed business while we were playing. We just enjoyed the day. Afterward, at the clubhouse, we usually had the opportunity to discuss business over a few drinks and a meal.

But directly talking business was not my goal. My goal was building a long-term friendship with Steve, which we still have to this day.

I think the goal should be to nurture the relationship first.

I think that's where people get it wrong; they want to share their product benefits first.

I realized that, nurturing a friendship with Steve on the golf course, it would eventually lead to referrals from him, and it did.

Steve sent business my way. He even became an advocate for me, educating his top clients on the benefits of using our manufacturing technology.

To this day, even in my own consulting business, I'm a firm believer in strategic partnering. It's one of the greatest ways to grow your business.

Building strategic partnerships can work in any industry, and it only takes two or three of these relationships to improve your business by 50 to 100 percent.

A financial planner can develop a relationship with a CPA or an estate planning attorney. A mortgage broker can partner with an insurance agent. A business consultant can partner with corporate sales professionals.

### *Action Steps for Developing Strategic Golf Partners*

Make a list of other businesses or professionals in your industry who offer noncompeting products or services, which complement your products or services.

Find out if any key individuals, within those targeted companies, play golf.

Contact the key individuals, within those organizations, and send them a formal invitation, by letter or card, to play golf. Let them know in the invite that the purpose of the meeting is not to sell or discuss any business deal, while playing.

Instead, let them know you are contacting them because you would like to get to know them, to determine if there is the opportunity for a mutually beneficial relationship.

Keep their interest in mind by letting them know you have clients who could benefit from their products and services.

In the invite, let them know you will be calling on a particular day to discuss scheduling a tee time.

Don't expect to get an answer right away; developing relationships takes time.

This is a process, which will likely require follow up, but, if you stay consistent, it will produce some impressive results over time.

Jonathan Taylor is founder of Buzz Mountain Media and author of the book: The Official Small Business Guide to Marketing 2.0. You Can Read his sales blog at: www.JonathanTaylor.tv.

# Creating Powerful Connections and Staying Top of Mind

■ Tim Davis

*"How did I make a twelve on a par five hole? It's simple. I missed a four-foot putt for an eleven."*

*- Arnold Palmer*

I got started way too late in playing golf and using the game to build my business. I had always heard that big deals happened on the golf course, but I simply resisted the idea.

Knowing what I know now, I hear Cher's song playing in my mind: "If I could turn back time."

Now, I am a sold-out believer that golf is an incredible way to create powerful connections for you and your business. I have also learned that it isn't about how well you play the game, but rather how well you connect with people. Isn't that the heart of business, today? Making connections with people who can, in turn, connect you with others.

I used to ask what someone's handicap was, prior to playing a round of golf, but today I ask this question:
"How many balls do you lose in a round?"

I have found this is a much better question when sizing up how the round may go, and I have also discovered that there are a quite a few business professionals who lose more than their fair share of golf balls in one round. For me, that is another connection point.

GetIntoGolf.com said, "Golf is perfect for building long and lasting relationships. There's plenty of time between holes for conversation – as well as a shared subject matter to chat about – making it perfect for forming long-lasting and genuine bonds."

Before I took up the game of golf, I made several excuses about why it was a waste of time. While the other sales professionals were at the course, I was back in the office making more calls. The real truth was that I believed the only people who played the game were semi-professional.

I let my inexperience keep me from the most important part of the game - the relationships you build. I can never emphasize enough the power of relationships in building your business. Bob Burg said, "All things being equal, people will choose to do business with people they know, like, and trust."

### How Connections Start the Ball Rolling

When you study how people first connect, you will discover that the majority of people initially connect over a common interest. For example:

Dog lovers will automatically have a connection with other dog lovers.
Fans of a sports team will automatically connect with other fans.
Golfers will automatically connect with other golfers.
Average, or below average, golfers really connect with golfers. ☺

This list could go on and on; however, at some point we have all experienced this type of connection. It is at that very moment, when you discover another person's passion for something is equal to your own, that a connection is forged. You may not know their political or religious views, but you know they love what you love, and, for the moment, that is enough.

My friend and mentor, John Maxwell, uses his book, Everyone Communicates, Few Connect, to say that connectors connect on common ground and that it increases your influence in every situation. I don't know of any serious, career-minded sales professionals who aren't passionately interested in increasing their influence.

Golf is a great way to break the ice and start the relationship building process. Right now, in your town, there is someone who could either use your services or put you in contact someone who does. That same person loves to play golf, but what they may not know is that you love to play golf, too.

My challenge to you, right now, is:

- Make a list of three prospects you would like to get to know
- Do some research to see if they like to play golf
- Call them to see if they would like to play a round with you
- Set up a tee time and play golf

Here is a special bonus: If you really want to take it to the next level and make a big impression, have a limo pick them up and bring them to the course.

### Building the Relationship and Making a Lasting Impression

I have learned that I'm playing golf to build relationships, not get sponsorships. Until NIKE or another major sponsor begins writing me checks, I am building relationships. The best way to build a relationship is to talk about FROG.

FROG stands for FAMILY, RELATIONSHIPS, OCCUPATIONS, and GOALS. In other words, spend time getting to know them. Everyone's favorite subject to talk about is themselves; your job is to let them. Be sure to make mental notes of what means the most to the other players. This will be important to remember, when you go to follow up.

I am not there to out-play the people I am with; I am there to build relationships. Who wins is irrelevant to me. I want to get to know them and see how I can serve them, but I am also there to make an impression. Because I am keenly aware that my golf game would not impress anyone, I have decided to go with my pants.

Many years ago, I was introduced to Loudmouth Golf. They make some of the most interesting patterns in golf attire you will ever see. At first I

was shocked. I thought Who in their right mind would show up to play golf in a pair of pants that looked like they had just finished painting a home, but I took the chance and became that guy. What I have learned in that by being "that guy" is that I make more connections.

Every time I play golf, I wear my Loudmouth pants, because, regardless of where I play, people come up to me and start a conversation. I intentionally stop at the grocery store on the way to the course, just to meet

more people. Zig Ziglar said that sales is a game of prospecting. The more people you can engage in a conversation, the more opportunities you create for yourself. Starting a conversation can be awkward, but it's never awkward for someone to come and talk to you.

The bonus is that the people I meet and play golf with, like to have their pictures taken, not with me, per se, but with my pants. I just happen to be wearing them. They then post these pictures on social media, which increases my visibility, brand, and, ultimately, business.

I'm not saying that you must wear outrageous clothing like me. Business is about relationships. Be great at connecting, even better at building relationships and your sales career will go far.

A four-hour round of golf is a great place to start.

"Fear comes in two packages: fear of failure, and, sometimes, fear of success."

- Tom Kite

"You don't close a sale; you open a relationship, if you want to build a long-term, successful enterprise."

- Patricia Fripp

# How To Grow Your Business, Build Relationships, and Help a Charity!

■ Joshua Lykins

I have worked in the golf business for 17 years, now. Every day yields a new discovery on how golf is helping me build my brand and increase revenue, all while helping others, too. Along the way, I have made some life-long relationships.

I played baseball, while growing up and all through elementary school, even into high school. One day, while I was living in Coral Springs, Florida, I was given the opportunity to volunteer for the local PGA Tour event as a standard bearer. My job was to carry a sign displaying the score of the professional golfers for the crowd following the group. As a typical teenager, I jumped at the chance to skip school for two days and hang out with celebrities.

I worked the 1996 Honda Classic for all four days. I was able to meet Greg Norman, Nick Price, Payne Stewart, Nick Faldo, Fuzzy Zoller, and many others. Little did I know, this decision would forever change my life in so many ways. It started me on what would become the career path for the rest of my life! I started playing golf on a regular basis, after that weekend. Two years later, I tried out for the golf team at my local high school.

After graduation, I went directly into the golf business. I took my Players Ability Test and passed on my first try. I, then, signed up for the PGA of America's Apprentice program. Over the next 15 years, I would work in the golf business for various courses across south Florida and middle Tennessee. The relationships I formed through the years have built my character and business to what is it today.

While working in the business and meeting professionals at the local country clubs, I began to notice a trend that was growing- and quite rapidly at that. Business and golf were going hand in hand more and more, and I started thinking of ways that I could incorporate my passion for charities into my work.

So in late 2012, I started an event management company called Elite Events of Music City. In years past, I had directed celebrity golf tournaments for a number of different organizations. All of these had been in my spare time and not under my business umbrella.

After starting Elite Events, I set out to try and secure events for the 2013 season and build what I hoped to be a successful business, which also benefited those in need. My first year went well and was a great success, even though I only had weeks to prepare myself for the season.

Heading into 2014 and my first true full year in business, with the golf season was just weeks away, I only had three golf tournaments booked.

I acquired all of these events from the people whom I had met on the golf course and through relationships I had developed over the past few years living in Nashville. With so few events, I was becoming stressed about how I would pay my bills and cover all of my expenses, as my previous year I used a savings slush fund, while growing my brand.

I thought long and hard about what I could do to make things progress and help me get new clients. One evening, I said a few prayers and spoke to God. I am not by any means a very religious person, but I turned to him and his guidance to make sure I was on the right path.

Over the next few weeks, I began playing in other charity events and helping out as many organizations as I could. I gave them free advice, and donated golf equipment and items to help raise money for their organizations through their auctions and drawings. I started meeting some great people in the local business community and building new relationships on a professional and personal level. Before I knew it, I had five new events and another three in the works.

Now having celebrity golf tournaments, concerts, corporate golf events, military balls, and other special events lined up, I was well on my way to a successful year in 2014. I was overwhelmed with the response from my new relationships and the trust they had in me to help them build their brand!

All of this was done while on the golf course, networking with others over a simple round of golf. I had just tripled my business in mere weeks! With my years of experience, I can now model an event budget and help my clients spend the minimal amount from their marketing budget (usually around one month's salary for an ENTRY LEVEL employee), and raise $10,000 or more for an organization close to their hearts.

While doing this, my client gets the publicity that would have come from their marketing budget anyway. It also brings their clients and friends together to create a unique networking opportunity in which everyone can benefit, regardless of their respective profession.

While all of this was happening to me, I met a man named Jaeson. I met him while playing in a charity event for Volunteers of America, through a former member of a country club I used to work for. Jaeson and I started chatting about a pair of shorts we'd received in our golfer gift bags.

This particular event had given out a pair of shorts from an up and coming clothing manufacture. The shorts we received were fun and festive, but hot and not the best of quality in terms of fabric and design. They also would have to be ironed every time you wore them, which is one of my pet peeves. I hate to iron!

We laughed about it, and chatted about what we would do to make it better and deliver a product that someone would want to purchase. Our conversation then turned to how we could do it and include charity, too.

Jaeson liked the idea of incorporating charity into the business and helping others. I knew things were on a great path! Through this round of golf, we chatted in depth about the clothing market, today, and what it would take to make something happen.

We exchanged numbers after the round and met up later that week to discuss things in a little more detail. This has led to our partnership in a brand-new clothing line called J2K Clothing Inc.

You never know where business will take you. Why not play golf till you find it? Whether you have never picked up a club in your life or just haven't been on the golf course in a while, make the time to get back out there. Invite some of your clients and friends. There is no telling what it can turn into after just a few hours of professional fun!

Today, I am very blessed and proud to say that I have a growing events business, here in Middle Tennessee, and that it is helping thousands of others in the process, through the nonprofit organizations I help raise funds for. The clothing line that is about to launch, and hopefully change the clothing industry by raising product quality to new heights, is another blessing that will touch the lives of many others.

Now, get out there and help build your brand and your future, one hole at a time!

FORE!


Hear a bonus audio interview with Joshua at: sellingonthegreen.com/joshua-lykins.

# Golf and Your Personal Brand

■ Dr. Deborah M. Gray

Personal branding is *how* you communicate your value. Golf can help you communicate your value much better than a Facebook page because golf takes place in person and over a significant period of time. That time can be used more efficiently if you know *what* you are communicating and *why* you are communicating it. I'm not suggesting that a Facebook page is not important to your personal brand, it can be, but I am suggesting that golf can help you build your personal brand in a way that digital media does not, up close and personal. To use golf as an element of your personal brand you must decide what you will verbally, nonverbally, and *intentionally* communicate on the golf course.

Brands create market presence and they build trust and confidence. Without a brand you are in a commodity market where price is the key determinate of who gets the sale. Personal branding is the process of intentionally and purposefully communicating *your* value. This chapter will give you a clearer idea of what a personal brand is, how to create one, and how to use golf to build and communicate it.

### Personal Branding

A brand is simply a value proposition that describes your unique position in the marketplace. Brands exist in the mind of the consumer but they are *built* by the marketer, or in this case, you. Whether you are aware of it or not, you are communicating your personal brand although you may not be doing it intentionally or purposefully. The

4-step process in this chapter will help you become more intentional and purposeful in communicating your value instead of just letting your personal brand happen incidentally.

Before we begin figuring out what your personal brand is, let me dispel a few misconceptions about personal branding. Personal branding is not personal self-promotion and it is not a logo. Finally, personal branding is not 'just your personality,' personal branding is your personal value.

## *4 Steps for Creating a Personal Brand*

Personal branding is the act of creating and communicating a unified message. It's up to you to determine what that message is and how you will communicate it. Four steps for creating a personal brand are 1) Identify your core values, 2) Define your personal brand purpose with a mission statement and a brand mantra, 3) Choose your brand elements and 4) Execute, evaluate, and adjust as necessary.

Your core values define who you are and what is important to you. The following is a list of core values compiled by Carnegie Melon University. Circle all of the words that apply to you; add additional words that you don't see but that come to your mind. If you spend more than 3 or 4 minutes on this, you are thinking too much.

| | | | |
|---|---|---|---|
| Abundance | Being the Best | Commitment | Dedication |
| Acceptance | Benevolence | Compassion | Dependability |
| Accountability | Boldness | Cooperation | Empathy |
| Achievement | Brilliance | Collaboration | Encouragement |
| Advancement | Calmness | Consistency | Enthusiasm |
| Adventure | Caring | Contribution | Ethics |
| Ambition | Challenge | Creativity | Excellence |
| Appreciation | Charity | Credibility | Expressiveness |
| Attractiveness | Cheerfulness | Curiosity | Fairness |
| Autonomy | Cleverness | Daring | Family |
| Balance | Community | Decisiveness | Friendship |

| | | | |
|---|---|---|---|
| Flexibility | Joy | Power | Success |
| Freedom | Kindness | Preparedness | Teamwork |
| Fun | Leadership | Proactive | Thankfulness |
| Generosity | Learning | Professionalism | Thoughtfulness |
| Grace | Love | Punctuality | Traditionalism |
| Growth | Loyalty | Quality | Trustworthy |
| Happiness | Mindfulness | Recognition | Understanding |
| Health | Motivation | Risk Taking | Uniqueness |
| Honesty | Optimism | Reliability | Usefulness |
| Humility | Openness | Responsibility | Versatility |
| Humor | Open-Mindedness | Responsiveness | Vision |
| Inclusiveness | Originality | Resilience | Warmth |
| Independence | Passion | Resourcefulness | Wealth |
| Individuality | Peace | Safety | Well-Being |
| Innovation | Performance | Security | Wisdom |
| Inspiration | Playfulness | Service | Zeal |
| Intelligence | Popularity | Spirituality | |
| Intuition | | Stability | |

Now that you have your list, I would like you to narrow your list down to 5 values that really capture the essence of who you are. With the 5 words on your mind, write 2 or 3 sentences that describe who you are and what you want to accomplish in your professional life. It is okay if you cannot integrate all 5 words into your sentences. You should take a few days or even a few weeks to reflect and hone what you have written until you are satisfied that those few sentences accurately reflect you and your purpose.

When you are done you will have completed step 2 and you will have translated your core values into a concise personal mission statement. One of the best personal mission statements that I've read is one written by Amanda Steinberg, founder of Dailyworth.com,

**"To use my gifts of intelligence, charisma, and serial optimism to cultivate the self-worth and net-worth of women around the world."**

Reading your personal mission statement every morning will keep you focused on your strengths and how those strengths will help you accomplish your goals. Another way to remain focused on your mission and purpose is to create a personal brand mantra –3 or 4 words that you should say in your head before every important meeting or decision. Brand mantra's are used internally and will not usually make sense to outsiders (as opposed to a tag line which is meant for others to hear and to remember). Your personal brand mantra will usually be said in your head or to yourself. If Steinberg's personal mission statement were your own, imagine that your brand mantra on the golf course or before other important meetings is "Smart, Charming, Optimistic." This is what you want to say, do, and reinforce while golfing with clients. If these three words are part of your value system the chances are good that you were already communicating them accidently, but what happens when you become more intentional about communicating your core values? The answer is that your clients will comprehend and remember who you are and why you are the person they want to do business with.

Creating a personal brand requires communicating and *reinforcing* your personal brand with brand elements (step 3), like golf. If you are reading this book it is a foregone conclusion that golf is, or will be, a part of your personal brand. Other elements of a personal brand might include a logo, a LinkedIn page, business cards, a web site, a tagline, or key words. My dad's tagline when I was a teenager was "nothing good happens after midnight." His value system was one of integrity, honor, and responsibility. My dad's words encapsulate him as a parent and quite literally condense years of communicating what is right and wrong, acceptable and unacceptable. A tagline is a good brand element to use while golfing—it is that thing that people remember that you say and they associate it with who you are as a person. If a tagline feels too forced for you, just get into the habit of *saying* who you are when you are *being* who you are. If you do that, you are branding yourself. Referring back to Amanda Steinburg's personal mission statement, she would be smart to remind her clients that she is optimistic when golfing by saying so and by behaving likewise. Develop some golf course actions that demonstrate your core values. Some examples of personal brand core values communicated through golf might be:

| Core Value | Golf Course Action |
|---|---|
| Thoughtfulness | Pick up the clients club for him/her |
| Preparedness | Bring items that others are likely to need or forget (tees, hand warmers, balls, kleenex, insect repellent, chapstick, sunscreen) |
| Family | Ask others about family and include your own family stories when appropriate |
| Daring | Take the risky shot and say something like, "I know this is daring but I'm confident it will work!" |
| Generosity | Tip well |
| Innovation | When you're taking a strategic shot say something like "I'm going to be really innovative here in the fairway, hit driver off the deck and cut it around these trees." |
| Integrity | Play honestly and fairly |
| Openness | Say something like, "What do you think Jim, I'm open for suggestions here" |
| Thankfulness | Mail a hand written thank you card after every round |

Here are a few tips for developing and communicating your personal brand:
- Synergy build brands faster and this happens when all of the elements of your personal brand communicate the same concise message.
- Keep brand elements to a manageable few. If you are using Facebook, LinkedIn, and Twitter, chances are none of them are at the level of excellence that they could be if you only had one of them to manage.

- Try to keep personal social networking separate from professional networking (Facebook for social, LinkedIn for professional).
- A LinkedIn page can be a great way to concisely communicate and reiterate your personal brand.
- Cross-reference your branding elements with each other (e.g. put your LinkedIn page on your business cards, put your favorite golf course on your LinkedIn page).
- Be mindful of unintentional negative personal branding, for example, an abandoned Facebook or LinkedIn page communicates inattentiveness.

The final step in the personal branding process is to evaluate and adjust. Create a "Why I'm Awesome" folder on your computer. Use this folder to store personal branding related files. Create a word document that includes your core values, mission statement, and brand elements. Add comments and reminders of what is working and what is not under each section of the document. Do this on a monthly basis so that you remain focused and what you want to communicate and what you are communicating. Don't be afraid to revisit and adjust your mission statement when your goals change or have been met. If you plan to use social media, make sure that your account is consistently active. Choose specific days each week to post and to attend to 'likes' and networking requests. Building your personal brand with purpose and intention will help you powerfully communicate who you are to your clients.

Dr. Deborah M. Gray is a Professor of Marketing at Central Michigan University in Mt. Pleasant, Michigan where she teaches marketing strategy and branding in a top-ranked MBA Program. She teaches a business course every spring in Scotland, United Kingdom where CMU students learn the value of building business relationships on the golf course while also learning about golf's deep historical and cultural ties to Scotland. She met and married her husband Trevor at Bucks Run Golf Course.

# Developing the Emotional Bank Account on the Green

■ Jonathan Taylor

> "People don't care how much you know until they know how much you care"
>
> – *Teddy Roosevelt*

In his classic bestseller, *The 7 Habits of Highly Effective People*, author Stephen Covey explained to us the importance of having a strong emotional bank account. We all love having a strong financial bank account where the deposits far exceed the withdrawals. An emotional bank account works the same way.

If I make continual deposits through empathy, kindness, honesty and keeping commitments, I begin to build up a huge reserve in the emotional bank accounts of my clients. Their trust in me grows to higher level each and every time. The opposite happens when I begin to take those relationships for granted. If I break commitments or fail to understand problems from the client's perspective, I risk making major withdrawals from the account. If this continues over time, the account can become overdrawn.

One of the ways we can make major deposits into those accounts is to "Understand the Individual". This seems simple enough but in reality, it takes a conscious effort. You see, other people's priorities are not our priorities; and you can't make deposits with others until you understand what is important to them.

Let me offer a quick story. Back when I was a sales executive selling raw materials in the composites industry, I had a buyer for a major account who I called on every few weeks. They were a great client, but there were still plenty of opportunities to sell them more materials for other manufacturing applications. So, I continued to work on building the relationship over time, meeting this buyer for lunch and sometimes dinner every few weeks.

As much as I pushed him to give us the opportunity to be his number one supplier, I couldn't seem to make progress. It wasn't until we started playing golf one day that things began to change. The first time we played golf, I was able to learn more about his everyday life, than I had ever learned over our one or two-hour lunch meetings.

One of the big things I learned as I asked questions about his family and his personal goals, was that he was really unhappy at his job. He felt he was getting underpaid for the increasing work demanded of him.

He mentioned that he had started looking for new opportunities with other companies.

"Great!" I thought. I'd spent all of this time building a relationship with someone who's about to leave.

I could have easily thrown in the towel after hearing this and stopped wasting my time with him if I were only concerned about my interests. But after weeks of playing golf and discussing life away from business, we had become more than just business acquaintances. We were friends, and I wanted to help him.

I immediately contacted the president of a manufacturing company that I thought was hiring for a similar position. This company was not a major customer but they did purchase from my company occasionally. As it turned out, they were hiring for the same type of position my buyer friend was looking for, and offering a much better compensation package. I put the two of them in contact with one another, and within a few weeks, he was hired for the new position.

The new job was a perfect fit for his talents, and also gave him double the salary he had been earning before. His new position even gave him more authority as a buyer and manager. He was so grateful for what I had done to help him that within a few weeks of starting the position, he called me and let me know that as the new buyer he was going to be sending all of their raw material orders to me, making me their one and only supplier and more than tripling my sales with them. I took this as a great lesson – "Seek first to understand".

You see, we often project out of our own autobiographies of what we think people want. We sometimes measure the emotional deposits based on what we think others need. In the case of this buyer, his real want and need was finding another job elsewhere. I wouldn't have discovered this without creating an opportunity to dig deep. To learn more about his personal life.

Golf is an experience that gives us as business professionals the opportunity to dig deep with others. To build trust through empathy. When it comes to long term sales relationships, it's hard to build those connections during a quick networking event or business lunch.

In his recent book, *Sales EQ*, author Jeb Blount says "When people feel connected to you, they feel more comfortable revealing their problems". It's hard to build that type of connection in a 1-2 hour meeting. On the golf course however, you have a longer more relaxing environment to build deeper relationships.

Be intention about growing that emotional bank account while enjoying the game of golf.

Jonathan Taylor is founder of Buzz Mountain Media, and author of four books including his recent bestseller Launch It: How to Use Videos, Podcasting, and Viral Marketing to Become a Recognized Expert in Any Industry. He is a veteran of the US Army, and uses his experience in the field of reconnaissance to teach winning strategies for prospecting & sales growth. You can follow his sales blog and podcast at www.SalesWarriorInc.com. Along with his passion for sales & marketing, Jonathan is an outdoor enthusiast with golf being one of his favorite sports.

# Advice for Mixing Business with Golf: Don't Do It

■ Bill Johnson

Early in my career, colleagues jokingly called me the "VP of Golf," because I spent so much time on the links.

When the weather cooperates, I like to get out to play golf a couple of times a week. I play golf sometimes for business and always for pleasure. Over the years, I've developed some very valuable friendships and business relationships with people who hit the links with me.

For this reason, it may come as a surprise when I tell people to never mix business with golf. If you do, you're going about it the wrong way.

Inviting prospects for an afternoon on the links solely to have the opportunity to sell them on your product or service will make for a very long and uncomfortable afternoon for everyone.

Instead, use the game of golf as a way to build a relationship with a prospect who may or may not turn into a business opportunity. Even if the business opportunity doesn't materialize, you will have made another friend and golfing buddy.

## The Mystique of Golf

Companies spend a lot of money and time entertaining customers and prospects, but nothing works to build solid relationships like playing a round of golf.

I simply can't think of another scenario in which a prospect would agree to spend four-plus hours with me in a social setting.

Unlike sponsorships and spectator sports, playing a round of golf requires everyone to participate. Golf offers the perfect opportunity to spend four hours outdoors, participating in a sport that everyone loves, while also getting to know each other on a personal level. In between tees, amazing discussions about family and life take place that just aren't possible in other settings.

One of my biggest deals came after nearly five hours on the golf course with an executive from Angie's List, a membership service that compiles consumer ratings of local service companies and contractors. While we were working on our Birdies and discussing our families, I never even mentioned business. Afterwards, over a drink, the Angie's List executive raised the topic of how my company, Salesvue, might help him improve sales.

The same thing happened years before, while I was playing golf with Dan Ariens, the CEO of Ariens Company, which manufactures lawn mowers and snow blowing equipment. Dan was vice president of engineering, at time, and we spent the first 11 holes getting to know each other. At the 12th hole, Dan complimented me on not talking business and then asked me about my company. He became a customer, and we remain friends to this day.

In fact, every executive with whom I've ever played golf has ended up becoming my customer and, more importantly, my friend.

### *Lessons from the Links*

There are a few lessons I've learned along the way about how golf can facilitate a great relationship, and how the day can fizzle out:

Don't use the outing as an infomercial. Golf should be the means to generate a personal relationship. The afternoon will quickly sour if prospects feel trapped by a prolonged sales pitch or feel they are the victim of a bait and switch.

Pick a course that's appropriate for the skill level of your guests. While most golfers would love to have the opportunity to play a championship course, inexperienced golfers will soon feel out of their league and the afternoon will deteriorate, if they are playing on a course above their skill level. I simply ask my guests for their handicap, when I invite them out. If they don't know their handicap, that's a good sign that they don't play often. If you happen to be playing a championship course and discover you're playing with an inexperienced golfer, shorten up the course to make the day less stressful. If you don't know the caliber of your guest, it's a good idea to pick a time that will allow you to play the course easily without feeling pressured by other golfers.

Keep foursomes to one company. Mixing prospects from different companies is awkward for everyone. The only common link is you, and that can make the day stressful. Instead, invite several executives from the same company to round out the foursome and schedule another golf date with the other company.

Finally, golf provides excellent opportunities to stay in touch with prospects. If I haven't communicated with someone in a while, I simply reach out and ask how their golf game is going, and that opens up the conversation again. Golf has the uncanny ability to cement relationships beyond the links.

Bill Johnson is president and CEO of Salesvue, a software solution that brings automation and insight to the outbound sales process. You can find out more about his company at www.salesvue.com.

Hear a bonus interview with Bill Johnson at: sellingonthegreen.com/bill-johnson.

"Golf is a matter of confidence. If you think you cannot do it, there is no chance you will."

- Henry Cotton

"Internalize the Golden Rule of sales that says: All things being equal, people will do business with, and refer business to, those people they know, like and trust."

- Bob Burg

# Success on the Golf Course Means Having a Plan

■ Matt Middendorp

Any sales person worth their salt will tell you that the cornerstone of sales success is building quality, lasting relationships. The beautiful part of that statement is, in the modern world, there are almost unlimited ways to connect with people on an individual level and nurture insight and trust.

Given the explosion of social media, networking groups, and events designed to facilitate this process, we sometimes lose sight of the obvious opportunities to bring people together in a less formal setting. Golf is a classic example of this type of environment. At its core, "the back 9" was made for building relationships and making deals happen.

I admit, it rarely surprises me when I'm working with a client who is an avid golfer, and they make a comment along the lines of, "I would love to take clients golfing, but my company won't pay for it." These clients are victims of the long line of sales people before them; the ones that take "prospects" (translated: friends who may or may not be legitimate prospects) golfing regularly, but rarely brought in new business from it.

Golf isn't the only business acquisition tool to be abused, but because it involves a larger investment in the sales person's time and the company's money, golf is easy to single out. My advice to clients that would like to use golf as a relationship building tool is simple, have a plan for the round, execute it, then be sure to share the results with your boss.

## The Plan

I recommend my clients use golf to build relationships in one of three ways

Building Relationships

Strengthening Relationships

Bringing People Together

### 1. Golf is a great tool for building relationships with prospects.

When I was in banking, one of my commercial bankers, Mike, was a master at using golf to build relationships with the right prospects. Here's a great example of some of the success that can be had on the fairways:

Mike had scheduled a round with a local developer who was planning a large building project. At the last minute, the developer called and let Mike know his father was in town, and asked if he could come along for their tee time? Due to the size of the opportunity, Mike graciously agreed. Over the course of the round, Mike took the time to build relationships with the father and son team, only to discover that the father was in the process of starting another large development project on the other side of the state.

Both father and son were so impressed with Mike, and the time he took to get to know them, that they both asked him to bid on their projects. In two and a half hours on the golf course, he secured two deals that capped off his goals for the year. Not bad for an afternoon's work.

## 2. Golf Is an Excellent Way to Strengthen Relationships with Existing Clients

I once ran a bank in a market that featured a large, regional medical facility. Yet, when I took a look at the bank's largest individual customers I noticed a lack of medical personnel using us as their primary bank. Sure, many of them had accounts, but it was clear the bulk of their money was being kept elsewhere. Recognizing the opportunity, we developed a strategy for growing our presence with the large number of doctors in town. We tailored our marketing program to appeal to them, including special products, discounts, and rates. We increased our presence on the numerous boards and fundraising committees at their facility. We started a special referral program for those who recommended co-workers to us. The expected lift never came. Then, one day, I was invited to go golfing by one of our doctor customers with some of his doctor friends, who also happened to be limited customers. Golf is a game of planning, persistence, and discipline; sales is, too.

My goal for the outing was to make three new friends. I researched the foursome on social media and the clinic website to learn more about them. I planned the questions and conversations we could have. Most importantly, I made sure none of it was about banking or finances and stuck to it. I'm going to admit something, it was really hard. I wanted so badly to pitch the virtues of the bank or ask their opinion on some of our marketing efforts, but I didn't, and it paid off. By the end of the round, I had three new friends, and by the end of the week I had three new committed bank clients. A winning customer acquisition strategy was born, and, ironically, over time, it proved to be our most successful.

## 3. Use Golf to Bring People Together

One of the keys to building deep, lasting relationships with clients is to demonstrate the value you bring, over and over. My passion as a sales consultant is to help businesses turn corners. Using my "Formula for Success," I teach individuals and teams how to sell, and managers how to manage them, but sometimes my prospects don't need a sales consultant. They have other problems that need to be solved.

Golf is a great way to bring together people who need each other but, for one reason or another, have never developed the necessary relationships to realize it.

Golf provides an atmosphere that is unmatched in the networking world. Business is being done, but, somehow, it doesn't feel like work in the golf cart. As someone who cares about my clients and their success, anytime I can help build a connection that helps their business meet its goals, then I meet mine as well.

### *How to "Win" The Round: Five Rules for Sales Success on the Golf Course*

1. Be a confident golfer. I'm not saying you have to be Jack Nicklaus, but the last thing you want them to remember from the round is your golf game.

2. Relax and have fun. If you are a confident golfer, try not to be a competitive one. I have golfed with good sales people who threw clubs when they shanked a drive or stomped and pouted on the way to the next tee box after 3 putting. You are golfing with clients and prospects to make a positive impression. Don't be "that guy" on the course that no one wants to be seen with in the clubhouse.

3. But not too much fun. Stick to a one to two drink limit on the course. When the weather is warm, the round is going great, and your company is paying for it, the temptation is there to forget the real reason you are driving in a cart instead of sitting at a desk. Discipline is an important part of golf. Forgetting your purpose can also ruin your chances with the important prospect you are golfing with. Bear that in mind,

each time the drink cart comes around.

4. Have a plan. Be sure to become an expert on your partners and their business before you hit the course. Think through possible conversations, and how to time them so your prospects will enjoy your company.

5. Be patient. My rule is simple, close deals on "the back 9" or in the clubhouse. First, build a relationship to create trust. Your partner, and pocketbook, will thank you for it.

In today's business world, there are endless options for connecting with your clients and prospects, and all of them work, when used properly. As spring rolls into summer, don't forget one of the classic relationship building strategies.

The next time you are facing a prospect that simply won't commit, or a mistake is made with a client, find a way to create the trust that you need to work together. Take them golfing.

Hear a bonus interview with Matt at: sellingonthegreen.com/matt-middendorp.

# How Golf Provides Opportunity for Woman in Business

■ Pam Swensen

As CEO of the Executive Women's Golf Association, I'm an avid proponent of playing golf for business. It's a vital tool that all salespeople should have in their skill set and an asset for anyone looking to advance his or her career.

I didn't grow up in a golf household, but I learned early on in my professional career that the game was a door-opener. The CEO of the telecommunications company I was working for tapped me to develop a sports marketing/client entertainment program in our region. The corporate entertainment program focused on developing engaging golf experiences for our clients that were captivating, inviting, and fun, with a purpose. I knew the importance of being able to walk the walk and talk the talk, and quickly looked for resources to accomplish just that.

At this same time, a new organization called the Executive Women's Golf Association had just formed in the Boston area. Professional women could come together, learn how to play golf, and develop a comfort level with the game. The ultimate goal was learning to use it as a networking tool for relationship building. For me, it was like winning the lottery!

When I started to play, like most women, I worried about embarrassing myself or other people with my lack of skill. I joined the organization in hopes of learning the game. EWGA helped me understand the basics and get started.

I put my foursome photos in my cubicle and kept current on the weekend tournaments results. This, essentially, gave me "water cooler" talk that was timely and of interest to my male colleagues. As the word got out that I was playing golf, I was looked upon differently by the senior level executives within my company. Invitations started to come my way to participate in charity golf events.

The golf course has been the setting for forging thousands of relationships, creating leaders, building potential business, revealing character, and closing deals. And, especially for women wanting to gain access into the "good old boy's network," learning to play "business golf" is a valuable and effective skill.

Statistics show that women who use "golf for business" close more deals because of the increased rapport and trust built playing golf with clients. So, whether you're an avid golfer or not and whether it's in your resume, or you have a photo of yourself playing visible in your office, make sure it's known that you can play. It's a great conversation starter and automatically establishes equality and credibility.

Little did I know, I would someday be leading this international organization and become its "voice for women's golf."

Golf reveals character. It's been said that golf brings out the best and worst in people. The game allows you to get to know your playing partners' personalities, outside of a work environment. It also allows your opponents to learn as much about you.

Situations created on the golf course reveal how you respond to success and failure; perform under pressure and how well you abide by rules and ethics. Many of the rules of golf apply to the business world and being successful at any endeavor.

Be prepared. The social skills in golf are just as important as the physical skills. It's important to take the necessary steps to adequately prepare for your business golf event. Make sure your guests have all the information they need in advance of the round - directions, tee time, dress code, locker room and practice facilities, course contact info, and any interesting information about the course design. Being prepared and on time is a major part of the day.

Pay attention. You can learn so much about yourself and your playing partners, during a round of golf. In every round of golf, there is something extraordinary that happens and something that's not perfect. It's humbling and a good test of character.

Some scenarios to consider on the golf course:

- How do you handle sudden changing conditions that require quick decisions? Are you indecisive and consistently spend too much time choosing a club or standing over a putt? Or are you prepared and always thinking ahead, taking several clubs to your ball in case the conditions are different when viewed up close?

- Do you make lots of excuses, such as noise during your back swing, or a gust of wind? Or do you accept the outcome of a missed shot and move on to the next task at hand?

- How do you perform under pressure? Do you have a temper? Have you ever thrown a club in anger? Or kicked sand in a trap after a poor shot? Outbursts of frustration reveal much about your temperament, which would seldom happen in a job interview.

- How well do you concentrate? Are you easily distracted or, worse, distracting? Do you check messages on your cell phone during the game?

- What's your capacity for fun? Can you laugh at yourself?

- Are you positive and helpful? Or only focused on your own game?

- Do you count all of your strokes? How ethical are you?

Remember your objective. It's important for you to know the etiquette of the game and have some basic golf skills, but business golf is about building relationships.

Stay focused on that goal and not your personal golf score. It is the interaction and insights that are gained while playing that will build the relationships critical to sales success.

Golf is a marvelous test of skill, competition, and character; the quest for continuous improvement; and includes moments of great exultation and, sometimes, huge disappointment. These characteristics are all key aspects in understanding business relationships, assessing leadership acumen, and influencing how clients and colleagues regard each other and, ultimately, if they want to do business together. As one top CEO said so perfectly, about the time it takes to play a round of golf, "If you can't close in four hours, then you can't sell."

I've been fortunate to build my career within the golf industry. Ultimately, it has opened doors for me, helped me build relationships among titans of the industry and among marquee players. It has enabled me to lead an organization that has touched the lives of more than 120,000 women in our twenty-three year history. The EWGA has been a crucial tool in making me more confident and in helping to enrich women's lives through the game of golf

"Confidence, in golf, means being able to concentrate on the problem at hand, with no outside interference."

- Tom Watson

"How you think when you lose, determines how long it will be until you win."

- Gilbert K. Chesterton

# How Golf Helps Women Gain More Sales through Relationship Building

■ Jennifer Harris

What if I told you that you could learn as much about a person in four hours on the golf course as most people learn in five years in the business world? Furthermore, executives who play golf make 17% more on average than those who don't? (The Economist, 2011)

Would you be more inclined to get out on the golf course?

I know I definitely would. Men all over the world have been playing golf for years, because the relationships they build on the course turn into better leads, more money, and bigger titles. They also play golf because they gain significant insight into their partner's character and integrity in a minimal amount of time.

Golf is the ultimate venue to build trust, open deals, and size up clients. For women to use golf as a business tool, they need to understand the basic principles. Once these are mastered, the game opens the door to increased sales and more clients.

### *Building Trust to Strengthen Relationships on the Golf Course*

To build trust on the golf course, you must do two things: have great etiquette and exhibit integrity. To do this, you need to focus on the following four things:

1. Be safe on the course
2. Respect your playing partners
3. Take good care of the course
4. Play fast

Exhibiting integrity is a whole other story, because you can't exhibit a great quality unless you already have it. Golf will only multiply your character defects or merit, thus highlighting your true self that could otherwise take years to uncover.

If you do have integrity, golf will make your strengths shine, and great deals will follow you from the golf course into the business world. The best way to exhibit integrity is by practicing good etiquette and following the rules. A man or woman who is willing to take a penalty on themselves is always someone you can trust.

## *The Golf Course Is for Opening Deals and the 19th Hole Is for Closing Them*

People always say that deals are done on the golf course, but I like to think of business golf as a place to open deals. A round of golf should be for enjoyment and getting to know someone, not necessarily talking specifics on a deal. We tend to like to leave that for the 19th or 20th holes, drinks after the round, or the follow up call or e-mail, respectively.

If we all go into a round of golf hoping to learn more about our playing partners, we will come out of it with an artillery of information that can be used as ammunition to close the sale later.

Imagine if you were out on the course with a prospect, and you found out he/she loves to surf. It just so happens that you have been surfing your whole life. You also have sons who are roughly the same age. Now, you not only have golf as a common interest, but you can set up a follow-up meeting, surfing with the kids. He or she is going to be more likely to work with you, because you are likable and trustworthy.

If you have to bring up business on the golf course, make sure to bring it up after the fourth hole. There is nothing worse than getting to the first tee box and someone asking you to tell them about your business. It throws you off your game before you have even started. I recommend the fourth hole because it gives you enough time to settle into the game and relax.

Once you are on the 19th Hole, business is fair game. There are two ways to go about closing the deal:

1. You brought the proposal with you and your partner was prepared for the whole presentation.

2. You talk about the proposal but set up a follow-up lunch or meeting to discuss the specifics.

### Size Up Your Client in a Half Day Instead of Countless Coffee Dates

As much as we want our clients to like us, we need to like them. There is nothing worse than going into business with someone who turns out to be a liar, cheat, or just plain difficult. If you play golf with them and follow my three secrets below, you will be able to determine if they are someone you want to work with. For this reason alone, I take all of my prospective business partners or collaborators golfing, before I go into business with them.

### 1. Ask Your Playing Partner to Engage in a Friendly Bet

This could be a quarter a hole, a beer, or just for bragging rights, but the way your partner responds to the request will speak measures about their security. If they will not bet, your playing partner is most likely insecure. They don't believe they can win and hates to lose. If they are super competitive and can't fathom losing, they will not react well to change and hardship. It's also a good indication they probably do not bounce back quickly from adversity. If they are willing to bet and have a wonderful match- win or lose- they are a keeper.

## 2. Keep Your Partners' Scores in Your Head and See How They React When You Question if the Score They Report Is Incorrect

If they say, "Wow you are so right! You'd think it would be easier to count to five," they have integrity. If they try to argue, then score is very important to them and may be more valuable than the bottom line in business. If they flat out lie about their score by not counting penalties and illegal mulligans, stay very far away from them in business, because you never know what else they are willing to lie about.

## 3. During a Scramble Tournament, See Who Takes Charge and Who Sits Back and Lets Them Lead

The man/woman who takes charge is a natural born leader. If they are great at bringing the whole group together by making sure each partner gets to use their shot, they are even more trustworthy. If they sit back and let others lead, it can be a great thing, too. They can see when someone needs to be the center of attention and in charge. These golfers and business people usually do a lot of the work, but never get acknowledged. Make sure you congratulate them, from time to time.

Now that you know how to build relationships and make more sales through golf, let's get you out on the course!

Hear a bonus interview with Jennifer at: sellingonthegreen.com/jenn-harris.

# Golf: A Game of Integrity, Dignity, and Enjoyment

■ Justin Follmer

For most of my life, I haven't personified the typical sports guy. You'll never find me quoting stats or knowing who the quarterback was for the Pittsburgh Steelers seven years ago. I don't watch hockey, baseball, tennis, or basketball. I watch one football game each year, the Super Bowl, and only because I enjoy a great, well-thought-out, marketing campaign- commonly known as a commercial.

Perhaps it's the MBA in me, or, perhaps, I have more important matters occupying my time. To each their own, right? However, the game of golf is slightly different. I do know some of the players, but I'm clueless as to their stats or even where they are from.

That doesn't matter to me. Golf is a game of integrity, dignity, and enjoyment. Take any one of those three principles away, and you're just chasing a white ball through some grass.

In my financial planning business, the days of selling are over. Goodbye Boiler Room. In fact, I don't even like the word "sell." I prefer to use "offer." I offer financial planning as a solution to financial problems.

I use the game of golf as a way to connect with and "feel-out" a potential client. I golf a lot with one of my dearest clients on Kiawah Island, SC, and he always says, "You know, Justin, you can tell a lot about a person just by the way they golf."

After thinking about it for a while, I realized that he had a brilliant point of view. If you operate your sales team the way that I run my business, you will find that qualifying your prospect is just as important as your prospect qualifying you.

Just like the Pareto Principle, also known as the 80/20 rule, you want to duplicate the 20% that gives you 80%. A sale is simply the product of a trustworthy relationship. In my opinion, it should be called Relationship Procurement, not sales.

You want customers who listen to you and trust your recommendations, just as your customers want quality products and services and appropriate action, when unexpected events happen. How you and your prospects golf will give each of you insight into each other's character. The way a person golfs speaks volumes to the way they will treat you and your associates.

If you shoot Par and mark Birdie on a hole, can you be trusted? Did you respect the game? Did your prospect play a drop and not count the drop as a shot? Is that an honest hole? Did you start the course with a nine iron and finish with a broken-over-the-knee nine iron?

Who has a temper when things don't go the way they envisioned? Is the general tone of conversation all about a player force-coaching another? Is there a Mr. Know-it-All in the foursome? Did you rake the sand after that awesome shot out of the bunker or leave it for the next person to take care of?

Think about some other scenarios that you may have witnessed. Now, think about that person trying to solicit you for business. I bet it would be tough to want to do business with that person. After all, first impressions do last a lifetime.

I was once a part of a mentor program at the college where I received my MBA. The program matched me up with an executive of a large manufacturing company. The goal was for these executives to become a positive role model for graduates.

He was a very successful young man. We met only once, and only once, for a reason. During our conversation, he mentioned that he would like to take me out golfing with him and a couple of his associates. Naturally, with me being an advisor, I thought this would be an opportunity to meet some prospects and have a great day on the course; perhaps it would be the beginning of what I thought would be a long successful business relationship.

He asked how I played the game, to which I replied, "I'm not that good, but I'm fun to be around, and I enjoy being out there on the course." His response was, "If you're not that good, then we're not interested in playing with you. We play to better our game and are very serious golfers."

Needless to say, that conversation ended my membership in the mentor program. Golf should be enjoyed. It's an opportunity to be away from the office and among our planet's greatest features. If you can't enjoy being among Mother Nature, then what are you working so hard for? Is the game really that serious, in the end?

Life is way too short to have a day "ruined" by a golf game. In fact, I would argue the opposite; any day I get to enjoy a game of golf is a great day, regardless of my score. Golf should be respected, however. Enjoy the game, yes, but not at the expense of respect.

I like doing business with people who show humility and respect towards other people and property. If you make a divot, fill it in. Follow the 90 degree rule, when in place, and wear appropriate clothing. Leave your jeans and t-shirts at home. Some of these things seem obvious, but I can't believe how many times I see these types of infractions.

Treat the cart girl or guy with respect, tip them well and even tip the maintenance team, if you see them on the course. I never pass an opportunity to thank someone for their hard work, especially in the sweltering heat of the South Carolina low country.

I always try to treat people the way I would want to be treated, if circumstances were switched. I believe you will find that great things will happen to your self-image, if you take on a similar persona. People want to do business with people who are generally good people, and these little things will set you apart from the rest. After all, how many times have you seen someone tip a greens keeper? It's that simple.

Generally, to be great at relationship procurement by using the game of golf, you must respect the game, be honest, and be a joy to be around. You have the ability to control your own actions more so than the actions of others. If you hold yourself to a higher standard, then you will attract others with a similar standard.

Business is solely based on trust, and the single best form of advertising is your existing clients inviting their friends to enjoy a respectful game of golf with you.

Justin M. Follmer, MBA, is an independent Investment Advisor Representative, with over eight years of experience in the financial services industry. You can find out more about Justin by visiting www.lowcountryadvisors.com.

Hear a bonus interview of Justin at: sellingonthegreen.com/justin-follmer

"I'm a firm believer in the theory that people only do their best at things they truly enjoy. It is difficult to excel at something you don't enjoy."

- Jack Nicklaus

"The secret of man's success resides in his insight into the moods of people, and his tact in dealing with them."

- J. G. Holland

# How to Use the "Little Birdie Strategy" to Let Your Prospects Know You Have the Best Product or Service

■ Rob Wilson

What's the best way to let your prospects know that you have the best product or service? Let a little birdie tell them. Ask anyone in sales, and they will tell you that word of mouth is the most powerful marketing method in the universe.

I've done seminars, speeches, lunches, dinners, social media campaigns, sponsorship deals-you name it. I've come to realize that nothing is more powerful than a referral from a satisfied customer.

When someone calls and says they "were referred by so-and-so," you know, immediately that the sales process is 90% complete. As long as you don't come off as a complete idiot on the phone, it's hard not to close new business when it comes in that way.

The problem is, even your most satisfied customers don't view their life's mission as helping you get more customers. Certainly, when someone asks them for a recommendation you'll be on their mind, but the frequency of that happening is pretty unpredictable.

Fortunately for you, there is a business tool used by many successful salespeople that can help you create an opportunity for strong referrals- golf.

Two great things about golf are that it can be played at any age, and, because only a small portion of the time is spent actually hitting the golf ball, it affords plenty of time to chat and build relationships. These conditions make the golf course a perfect environment for growing new business.

As with any game, there are strategies you will want to employ to give yourself the best chance of winning, especially when you are trying to win over a new prospect that hasn't done business with you yet.

Consider me your personal Butch Harmon of business and allow me to introduce you to my "Little Birdie Strategy." While it's true that golf affords you a significant amount of time to talk with people you'd like to do business with, no one wants to subject themselves to four hours of how great you are.

Any hint of that and you'll never be able to put a foursome together. There are better ways for you to get your message across subtly. Let it come from a source with much more credibility than you: The Little Birdie.

Here's how it works:

### *On the Course*

Put together a foursome that includes you, your prospect, one of your best and most satisfied clients, and one person that you think your prospect would like to meet.

Don't do what most people do and sit in the cart with your prospect so that you can talk his or her ear off. Make sure that the course knows to put your prospect and your best client in the cart together.

Done correctly, you may not have to make one single "pitch" the entire round. Why? Well, as they ride around the course together, the question, "How do you know Rob?" will inevitably come up.

As your client describes your relationship and the great work you've done for her, your prospect not only gets a live testimonial of your professional prowess, but also gains access to someone to whom they can ask questions about how your product or service might benefit them.

In this way, it's like having a "little birdie" chirping in your prospect's ear, throughout the round. Certainly, they will discuss other topics, but your name and business will come up. When it does, the little birdie will tell them all they need to know.

### *Ask and You Shall Receive*

Your job is not to talk but to listen. You are still selling, even when you are not extolling the virtues of your business. The best salespeople aim to know what's most important to their customers and prospects, what their pain points are, and how they can best solve their problems.

There's no better way to get this information than to spend time with someone on the golf course. But you must be truly engaged and interested in what your prospect has to say. Ask the right questions. Ask about their family. Ask about proud moments in the last year. Ask thoughtful questions, and you'll have more than you'll need to craft the proper pitch, at the right time.

Keep a notebook with you and write down key things about your prospect that you'll want to remember. Don't worry, it will look like you're taking notes on the course or reviewing notes on your swing.

### *After The Round*

Your little birdie can be helpful in this area, too. After the round, ask your long-time client how the conversation went with your new prospect. What did he or she learn? Did they find anything particularly interesting?

Chances are your prospect and your long-time client discussed life, family, business, politics, the weather and more, at some point during the round. Use those insights to determine if there is something you can do to show your interest in your prospect. Send them a relevant article. Mail them a book. Introduce them to someone.

### *Show Them That You Care, and You're Not Just out for another Sale*

Don't be lazy. If nothing else, you must at least send a handwritten (not e-mailed, Tweeted, Linked-In-ed, or Facebooked) note, thanking your prospect for spending time with you and your group. No one does this anymore. You'll stand out.

Try the Little Birdie Strategy the next time you're looking for a way to grow a new prospect. Even if you don't have any Birdies on your scorecard, you might just end up with a hole-in-one for your business.

Hear a bonus interview with Rob at: sellingonthegreen.com/rob-wilson.

# Why the ROI on a Well Planned Round of Golf is Significantly Higher than Most Marketing Tactics Companies Use

■ Ken Cook

I have a confession to make, right up front – I'm a golfer. I've played for over 35 years, and, last year, I broke 80 for the first time. I did it only once, but it's enough to ensure I'll be back for years to come.

I tell you this so you understand that I have a built-in bias when it comes to golf. However, that bias does not diminish my recommendation – play golf to build relationships. Golf is an uninterrupted four or more hours of conversation, banter, and opportunities to get to know someone.

I recommend this because relationships are rapidly becoming the only truly sustainable differentiation. Today, the solutions-oriented salesperson is a commodity salesperson, because everyone is doing it. Customers expect that, when a salesperson crosses their threshold, they need to bring more than just solutions to the table. The customer's expectations are that the solutions will be the baseline for consideration.

Add to this the world of instantaneous access to information, and we have customers who are almost as well informed as the salesperson as to what solutions are available. If a customer doesn't know the answer, a simple online query to Google or a question posted on a myriad of social network platforms will invite more information than the customer really ever needs.

Solutions by themselves are no longer unique. At the decision table, the customer has multiple, equally promising solutions from which to choose. Thus, their decision is based on emotions, with the emotion of trust dominating the process. Trust only comes from a relationship; in today's world, the relationship with the customer is the differentiating factor.

My business, How To WHO, Inc. (www.howtowho.com), is all about how to build relationships and leverage them to increase business. Everyone in business agrees that relationships are important. I even saw a columnist in the Philadelphia Business Journal declare that 2014 is The Year of the Relationship.

It's important to understand that building relationships entails going beyond the recognition that relationships are important. You need to understand how to build a relationship, and that requires some work. The work involves understanding the dynamics of how people interact, as well as mastering interaction skills that keep the relationship positive and collaborative and applying interaction tools that assist in moving interactions forward in a collaborative and supportive way.

The challenge we all face is the commitment of time and effort needed to build relationships. Many companies might think it a waste of time and resources. After all golf, at a four hour minimum, takes a long time.

From a strictly business and financial perspective, in my opinion, the ROI on a well-planned round of golf is significantly higher than most marketing tactics companies use. It is time well invested.

If you consider the typical sales funnel, a company would put 100 suspects into the top of the funnel and be happy with two to five qualified prospects and proposals as a result. At best, the company earns a 5% ROI.

With a round of golf, you have an opportunity to connect to someone and really build a relationship with them. You are in an environment where you have someone's attention, without the normal wide array of distractions.

Most importantly, golf is not about business; it's about getting to know the person and building some trust between you. Golf is a social event; it is a competitive event; it can be a team event; it tests character; it tests patience; it can reveal flaws; it can highlight strengths. You have opportunities to really get to know someone and connect with them in ways a business meeting would never afford you.

Let me finish the ROI discussion with some examples: A good friend of mine is the managing partner of a financial services firm. He plays golf as his primary marketing tactic. Over a nine month season in Rhode Island, he probably plays 75 rounds of golf. When he plays, he usually invites people he knows, but who don't know the others. He's generous with his relationships, connecting people who would benefit from knowing each other.

He also keeps track of every round on a spreadsheet. It is not unusual to get a call months, or even years, after a round, where someone with whom he played asks for the name of someone else in the group. "Fred, who was that banker we played with last year at the Chamber event?" Fred quickly reconnects the people, because his spreadsheet has all of the information.

The ROI argument for Fred – his business grows every year. He never makes a cold call. Every new piece of business comes to him through a warm introduction. Fred's close rate is well over 50%, which is considerably higher than a 5% close rate.

What Fred did is turn the typical sales funnel into a sales megaphone. Rather than winnowing down suspects to prospects to deals, Fred focuses on his relationships and leverages them for more of the same. His fans happily connect him to people with whom he builds relationships, trust, and, eventually, business.

Let me share one other short example: I had a good relationship with a Senior VP of a strong, national bank. I did not know the Regional President. I arranged a golf outing, which was the beginning of a relationship with the Regional President. Within six months of the outing, we were doing a $25,000 project for the bank, and, just as important, the relationship with the Regional President afforded me introductions to his peers around the country. A local relationship, built on trust, is evolving into a national account.

The position that there is a stronger ROI through relationships can be substantiated by story after story. The role golf can play in helping build relationships is equally evident. Remember, though, that golf is a "relationship building zone." It is not a "selling zone."

Relationships and typical selling are like oil and water. In typical selling environments, the motivations to persuade and convince someone to do business with you take over. Also, when someone tries to convince you to do something, the natural reaction is to put up defenses. The interactions become contentious and self-protecting, not collaborative and supportive.

Relationships are not something you can create out of thin air when you need them. You need to build them before you need them. Initiating and strengthening your relationships takes time. Like Rome, trust is not built in a day.

Think strategically, focusing on relationships that are going to strengthen and benefit both sides. Make informed choices when selecting those relationships. Then invest time in order to build trust.

And as sacrilegious as this phrase might be, realize that your investment does not have to be golf. Find activities that become part of your normal schedule and routine. Examples could include:

- Host a dinner once a month and invite three people with whom you want stronger relationships. Make sure the three people would benefit from knowing each other.

- Every week set aside one hour to call at least three people whom you haven't spoken to in a while. Inquire as to how they've been and look for a way to be generous or to help.

- Once a week make an e-mail connection between two people you believe should know each other.

- Forward an article of interest or a send an interesting book to someone.

- Use your electronic calendar skills to remember birthdays; be different and remember anniversary dates as well (for anything memorable, not just marriages).

Each of the above activities is about generosity and getting to know someone outside of the strict confines of business. So, whether it is golf or something else, build a set of activities that are uniquely you. Choose things that reflect your style and how you connect with people.

The key is making sure you invest the time, today and tomorrow. When you need a relationship to help you, it will already be there. You won't have to go looking for it or hope to build it.

Hear a bonus interview with Ken at: sellingonthegreen.com/ken-cook.

"Golf is deceptively simple and endlessly complicated; it satisfies the soul and frustrates the intellect. It is, at the same time, rewarding and maddening - and it is, without a doubt, the greatest game mankind has ever invented."

- Arnold Palmer

"To succeed in sales, simply talk to lots of people, every day. And here's what's exciting – there are lots of people!"

- Jim Rohn

# How One Round of Golf Can Reveal Everything
## You Need to Know About a Potential Client

■ Dan Pincus

As a child and young adult, golf was foreign to me. My impression of the game was to wonder who are those crazy people (playing in both good and bad weather and wearing unusual clothing)?

As someone who always thought sports involved running games, not walking and hitting a ball, golf did not appeal to me. Besides, my friends were not golfers, so that was a big reason for me to not even consider playing the game.

Fast forward to an interview with a manufacturing company that had just hired me to run their sales and marketing:

The president asked me, "You play golf, right?" My answer, of course, was no. His reply to me was very jarring, "You have three months to learn the game, no pun intended, but if you can't play golf, you have a handicap, running sales and marketing for our company." Well, as any responsible employee would do, I started playing golf. I was terrible; however, I was told early on: it is not how well you play that matters; it's knowing the rules and etiquette, and how you play the game that matters most.

The owner believed in the power of golf as a business tool so much that every Monday he had all his employees play golf. (We would leave the office at 1:00 p.m., every Monday, from April to October, to play 9 holes of golf at a local golf course). Every employee would play with every other employee (in different foursomes), and we all kept track of every stroke we took (even if we missed the ball, moved the ball, or made a mistake).

Scores were kept and tallied, and people knew who had the most Pars, Birdies, etc., and, also, we would see how our score improved, or fell off. As a competitive person, I was embarrassed that I had over 100 (on 9 holes) when I began playing. However, I was proud that I brought my score down to the low 50s by the end of the first golf season. What was very interesting was that I really bonded with all the employees that golf season. I got to know the people in finance, operations, and, even the administrators. This was the logic behind the president's actions (of losing four hours of productivity per week, seven months a year). He felt that the employees would work better, if they knew each other and understood what they each had to go through to get their job done).

Many days, I would go out with the president to his private golf club for lunch. Before lunch, we would always stop by the putting green and play about 15 to 20 minutes (betting 10 cents a hole). During this time, he would teach me why golf was so important in business.

He explained to me that golf was always used as a tool to know who you were dealing with. It takes away all the cover ups that people use to portray themselves (as they think others want to see them). The president would tell me that people can hide who they are over a lunch or drinks. Sometimes, they can hide who they are, even when working with others for months or years. But one round of golf will show off all their secrets (if you know what to look for).

Here are some examples:
- Are your golf partners truthful about their golf scores? If not they may not be truthful in business.

- Do your golf partners follow the rules and etiquette of the game? If they don't, they probably have little respect for you and the game of golf. It also shows that they may be sloppy when details come into play.

When playing golf, you are going to see how this person communicates with you and the others in your foursome. You can see how he/she would act with other employees, how he/she would speak with potential clients, and, in general, his/her true nature.

When your golf partner hits a stray ball (hooks it or shanks it) to the woods or to an undesirable location, how do they react? Do they curse? Do they throw their clubs? If they brush it off with a laugh, you can be sure that they won't stress over problems at work. However, if their attitude changes over a few bad shots, you can bet that they will be hard to deal with when things go wrong at the office.

There are other things you can learn about a person on the golf course. However, the main fact is that: four to five hours on the golf course will help reveal whether this person would make a good employee, good client, or, in general, someone you would like to build a relationship with.

After leaving that manufacturing company, I worked as a vice president of sales and marketing for other businesses and began tracking how business was coming in. I was surprised to see that golf was, undeniably, the best way to grow business. More than 50% of the qualified people whom I invited to play golf became clients.

The hard part was not having them become clients; it was getting them to agree to play golf.

The reason is that most people don't have a problem playing golf with potential clients. They do, however, have an issue playing golf with vendors. As you can imagine, they want to be productive in bringing new sales to their company, and, although it is good to know your vendors, few people see the need to play golf with them.

After experiencing this through many different companies, I decided to seek a service that would use golf to connect me with potential business associates.

I could not find one, so I decided to create a business that would do this, as well as speed up the business development process. World Golf Network was created in 2003 and helps facilitate executive meetings with relevant people who will help them grow their business.

Hear a bonus interview with Dan at: <u>sellingonthegreen.com/dan-pincus.</u>

# What's Behind the Pink Tee

■ Terry Coleman

My dad introduced me to the greatest game ever when I was eight years old. Little did I know then how much golf would influence my life.

Growing up, I loved participating in competitive sports. I played every team sport I could, but I was always drawn back to golf. In team sports, someone was always pointing a finger at someone else and blaming them for the team's success or failure. With golf, it is you playing against the course – not your opponent. Like business, you get out of it what you put in it.

The first thing my dad did when teaching me the game of golf was to give me a copy of the rules and etiquette. He told me to read and memorize them.

Over the years, I've referred to those lessons many times and have found them to be especially useful when conducting business on the course. They teach you to respect others as well as yourself.

As I got more into the game, I wanted something to separate me from the pack; something that would be memorable. I used to help my dad out at the golf course where he worked. Back in the 70s, tees didn't come prepackaged. They came loose in a box of 50,000. It was my job to bag them up, 15 tees per bag. I noticed that grown men had a phobia about the color pink. They didn't want to buy the bags with pink tees. So, I decided to separate the pink ones out and use only pink tees when I played.

After I started doing that, people noticed and started ragging me about it. That was exactly what I was looking for. The pink tees became one of my trademarks. Over the years, it's been the start of many conversations. As time went on, I wanted to add something to go with the tees. So, I started wearing bright colors that other people wouldn't wear. Between the tees and clothes, I was remembered. To this day, people I have met and played with comment on my use of pink tees.

When I was growing up, I had a friend who made fun of me more than most for playing golf. He didn't think it was a hard enough game. He would say, "The ball is just sitting there, and you hit it." In the end, I got the last laugh. He had been at UT for about three weeks when he called me one day to ask if I would meet with him to teach him about golf. I asked why he suddenly changed his mind. His reply was, "My major is business management, and my professor told the class, we needed to learn to play golf; it will help us be more successful in business."

## *20 Tips for Using Golf to Improve Your Business*

1. Going to the course and being paired up with other people is a great way to meet new people and have four hours to get acquainted.
2. I like using the FORD philosophy to start conversations: F-Family, O-Occupation, R-Recreation, D-Dreams. You already have a common interest. By using this, you find out more about the person.
3. Always make sure you have business cards.
4. Don't cheat. Play the game as it is meant to be played – by the rules. It doesn't make a good impression if you cheat to save a stake or two on the course. It would make me wonder what you would do in the business world.
5. If you invite or are invited by a client, be on time. Early would be even better.

6. Don't be too competitive. You are there to build rapport and trust with your playing partners.

7. To wager or not to wager? Wagering is integral to golf and is a good way to build camaraderie. Keep the wager friendly and the stakes low. The most common side bet is a Nassau (three bets for the round – the low score on the front 9, on the back 9 and on the full 18). Set the dollar value low, making sure to keep it fun.

8. Don't make excuses for your game. It is important to know the etiquette of the game. If you are new, don't be afraid to acknowledge that and welcome any tips.

9. Control your anger. Don't curse and throw your clubs.

10. Remember to compliment your partners on good shots and putts.

11. If you have logo golf balls from your company, be sure to offer a sleeve or box before teeing off.

12. If you know the course and your partners do not, be sure to offer pointers on the areas to avoid on each hole.

13. Structure the outing so you have time for lunch or a happy hour visit after the round. This time affords a better opportunity to discuss business.

14. Be on your best behavior. Golf is a most revealing activity. Your true personality is going to come out. Are you a cheater, or an honest, generous person?

15. Take it easy on the alcohol. You always want to remain in control. I personally don't drink while on the course. I am there to do my best. Especially don't drink if your partners aren't drinking.

16. Treat everyone you come in contact with like gold. Even if someone really upsets you, address the situation with a smile and without getting loud. When a client sees how you handle yourself under pressure, it will go a long way. Treating the

employees at the course well is also an indication of your favorable character.

17. Pick a course you both will enjoy. Do your homework on course conditions, such as aerated greens or course or club house construction.

18. Let your client choose which tees to play from. Be prepared to play to the comfort level of your companions and guests.
19. Observe dress codes. Don't show up in cargo shorts and a tee shirt. Wear nice shorts or slacks and a collared golf shirt. If you are a guest of your client and they are a member of a country club, ask your client or call the club to ask if they have

a club house dress code. Some clubs require a sports coat to go outside of the pro shop.

20. Respect the etiquette of the game by repairing divots on the course, ball marks on the greens and raking bunkers if needed. These are small details that clients will notice, because they show respect for both the course and the golfers behind you. Stand away from fellow players and out of their sightlines when they are playing a shot. A moving shadow during a swing can be an unwelcome distraction. By all means, be quiet during the swings of others.

The bottom line is that a golfing occasion should be fun, even when your business colleagues are present. Be mindful of the behaviors you demonstrate while golfing and the experience may lead to some the most treasured times your business and personal life.

"Some people think they are concentrating when they're merely worrying."

- Bobby Jones

"Sales are contingent upon the attitude of the salesman, not the attitude of the prospect."

-William Clement Stone

# The Consequences of "Hard Selling" During Golf

■ Scot Duke

*The Soft Sell*

A soft sell occurs when the business's product/service information is indirectly offered to a person, without applying any pressure on them to take any action.

A soft sell is more of a passing of information on the products or services a business offers.

One of the best examples of how not to handle business on the golf course took place in Las Vegas. I was celebrating my wedding anniversary and playing golf with my wife. We had a tee time early one morning. There was a group in front of us at the tee, and they had a little staging area for us to stay back about 100 yards from them, until it was our time to come to the first tee. So, I got to watch the whole drama from this group unfold right in front of us.

I knew from overseeing so many rounds of golf what I was looking at would probably be a train wreck, because one of the guys was there in a suit and the other two guys were in their shorts. The suited guy looked like he was their butler or something! He was riding in the golf cart by himself with this big Rodney Dangerfield looking golf bag.

The other two guys were obviously the better golfers. We saw that from the first tee. They wanted to play from the middle tees and he wanted to play from the back, but, when he went back there, he couldn't hit it past the woman's tee.

This went on for a couple of holes, but all during this time, he kept going back to his cart and pulling out pieces of paper and getting in the cart with the other two guys while they're waiting on the group in front of them to hit. I knew he was talking business.

This lasted all the way through the entire front 9. As we got to the 10th, the guy got out his briefcase and started pulling out all these contracts.

All of a sudden, we saw three golf carts of caddies coming down the cart path towards that hole. They put the guy in one of the carts and escorted him out to the parking lot.

My curiosity was really peaked, and I had to find out what took place. When we arrived at the club house, we sought out the other two guys who were sitting, having drinks. They waved me over and said, "Listen, we want to apologize for the incident. We know we were holding you guys up; it was the idiot who was with us."

I said, "Yeah, what happened there?" One of them replied, "Well, we're an engineering firm. We do large building constructions, and this guy was from Chicago. He's an agent for building brokerages, and they had a building that it they wanted us to bid on in Chicago. We wanted to meet in Vegas because we're from California, so he said let's just meet in Vegas, and we'll talk about the contract.

"When we got to the 9th hole, this guy got a phone call from his boss, who told him to go ahead and get that contract signed now, and get on the next plane back."

So, he wanted them to go ahead and sign the contract. But they had told him during the front 9 that they were holding people up, and that they would talk business after the game. This agent's boss wouldn't have it, though.

So, they called the house and said, "Can you come and pick this guy up?" And they did. They ushered him right off the course.

The two bought my wife and me a drink, apologizing again for the hold up.

That was the worst case of boardroom that I have ever seen.
One of the best examples of business golf, done the right way, happened with a current business partner, Dave Bisbee:

Dave was in the PGA, and he had been out on a speaking tour, talking about how to use golf as a business tool.

We met online and, through mutual admiration, we agreed to go play some golf.

I actually had a chance to go out to Phoenix Arizona, where he was located, and took a week to play golf with him. We had a great time.

We didn't talk business. He didn't teach me golf, as golf instructors sometimes like to do. He treated me as somebody he wanted to get to know.

It was a time to be out there to get to know each other. And that's a great example of how business golf should work. We formed a very nice partnership, and it's still very robust.

We're both very dedicated to bringing the benefits of golf to the attention of the golfing world by using golf as a real business tool and not just something that is part of an automatic sales contract.

It's a success story because I didn't know what was going to come from our time on the golf course. I was focused on depositing more into that solid business relationship account.

I didn't want to try to sell anything; I wanted to see if this was going to work. When you go into business with somebody, the worst thing to do is go into business with the wrong person.

I left there with a 50/50 feeling on how things went. Two weeks later, he contacted me and said, "Hey, let's do it, let's go ahead and do it."

I thought things had gotten cold, but he came back, and he was really motivated. It was really one of the biggest personal success stories I've had on the golf course.

### *Some Tips for One-On-One Golf Outings*

Over 60% more business relations can be developed by using golf as a networking tool, more than any other, conventional, business-networking gathering.

Call up a valued customer and invite them to play a round of golf.

The best thing to remember about playing golf with a business client or customer, is that golf has natural ways to building amiable relationships built into the game.

Used correctly, this part of the game can be build a solid, personal relationship. And most people would rather do business with someone they know and like.

Keep these in mind when developing the plan for a one-on-one golf outing:

- A formal invitation should be part of the plan. Too many times, the invitation to a round of business golf is too vague in what is included, or hints at being a casual affair.
- The casual statement: "Let's play golf," while mixing in a business social environment should be backed up immediately with a phone call or e-mail.
- If the golf outing is to a charity golf tournament or some other organized golf outing, a printed invitation would be more suitable and appropriate. Printed invitations have a better response and generate more interest.

- Make a deliberate effort to be clear in the invitation that cocktails and dinner are included after the round of golf. There is no need in being overly detailed in the invitation; just make it clear that there is an expectation of an after golf gathering. Your guest will then know there is an expectation of sticking around after the round and can schedule in the time needed to enjoy the day.

- It would be appropriate to add a remark during the closing of the invitation of saying something like: "Look forward to playing golf and speaking with you on (just a very small tidbit of information on a subject you want to discuss), after our day on the course." This lets them know there is some expectation of talking after the round, and being up front will eliminate misunderstandings and relieve the pressure from your guest wondering what is intended. The best plan is to let your guest know what the plan is.

## *The Foursome*

Sometimes it is good to have a small group for a round of business golf. It can be helpful to have a regular foursome to frequently play with. A foursome is a manageable number and creates the opportunity to spend quality time with each person while out on the course.

Remember, the more time spent playing golf with someone, the greater the deposit into the Solid Business Relationship Trust Account.

Each round of business golf results in a higher balance in the SBR Trust Account, generating a greater possibility of a large return on your investment.

The business has to be managed, as does golf. Here is how to manage the uses of golf as a way to do business:

## *The Plan*

Many business owners or executives are good in business and want to be good in golf, or the other way around. These business golfers, more than likely, became good in business because they know how to develop a plan and stayed with it. The same goes with using golf to do business.

In order to manage business or golf, there has to be a plan.

The plan should be made, before you get to the course, or, even better, before making the call to invite someone to play business golf.

The plan should outline the purpose of the outing and what is to be accomplished. Most of the time, the purpose is to just get away and play golf, which is quite all right, too.

Always have something to be accomplished from the round, even if the goal is to have fun and break 100. State that as the plan and go for it.

If it serves a greater purpose or feels more comfortable to have a business purpose, then think about exactly what is needed or wanted from the round of business golf.

The purpose could be:

- To get to know a new client
- To get feedback from a valued employee
- To network services, through a vendor

Once a purpose has been established, what needs to be accomplished becomes crystal clear.

Set simple goals to reach the purpose.
For example:

- Learn three things about what's important to the prospective customer.
- Ask questions during the round that lead up to the goal.
- Write out a simple and easy plan and make a timeline, outlin-

ing the entire day, but do not make that information known to your business golf partners.
- Playing golf comes first, and business issues should be secondary.

## The Invitations

Produce a formal invitation to send to each guest. If the outing is just for a few business clients, adapt the plan accordingly.

If the entire group knows each other, the invitation can be more casual. If the golfers do not know each other, then include ample time before the round of golf, so that all players can get to know each other before starting.

Whichever style or formality you chose, make sure to send a printed invitation to each of the guests.

An invitation, mailed to each person, is the most effective way to organize a round.

E-mail will work if the guests have accepted a previous invitation, but if the players do not know each other, make sure to send each person an individual e-mail. A mass e-mail can be used if they all know each other.

Make sure to mention all of the names of the players on each invitation.

When addressing a group, make sure to let them know they are all invited to cocktails and dinner.

Again, being up front with the guests will greatly improve the likelihood of your gathering providing improvement to your business network.

## *The Follow-Up*

The most important part of a round of business golf is the follow-up. If the round was successful in accomplishing the goal, the follow-up becomes a natural part of the process of building a solid business relationship.

The follow-up from a round of business golf is an opportunity that no other activity can offer. If the round was played correctly, the host should have made a large deposit into the SBR Trust Account.

The host's integrity has now been established, and the guests are more than likely to look forward to the follow-up contact.

The follow-up should be made with the same seriousness that went into developing the invitation.

The follow-up should be:
- A printed Thank You card
- An e-mail
- A phone call
- A text message
- Or, if convenient, in person

What the follow-up does is simple: it shows integrity. A quick note or call to each golfer secures a lasting relationship.

The follow-up is like receiving the receipt to the deposit made into each person's SBR Trust Account.

Hear a bonus interview with Scot at: sellingonthegreen.com/scot-duke.

# How to Create Memorable Experiences on the Golf Course for Your Clients

■ Eli Goodrich

Golf is a great equalizer for a business relationship. Memorable bonds are built by removing a potential adversarial relationship and replacing it with the common ground of shared experiences. A round of "customer" golf is where people can meet and enjoy many hours together, thus setting a communication tone that breaks down barriers.

Golf most likely is not an opportunity to close big sales. Completion of a sales cycle is accomplished via the various operational elements with purchasing, legal, pricing teams, and business users. In general, "closing" a deal is best left for a business meeting. Golf is a great accelerator to either launch a business relationship, deviating from the traditional "seller vs. buyer" conflict or to build upon an existing bond, by moving the discussion from the office to the enjoyment of the event.

Let me share a couple of memorable examples.

I had been working to convince a CEO of a multi-national company to adopt a platform I represented. For two years, he resisted taking the final step and directing his VP to organize and purchase. We did, however, have occasion at two different off-site conferences to golf together. We had an enjoyable time and our common ground became golf and our rounds together. He was well aware of what I was selling and I was cognizant of his reluctance to commit.

We both were attending a conference in Beijing. He was an attendee and I was an exhibitor. Many people were bringing their clubs for the conference golf tournament. I reached out to him and suggested we also take an extra day to golf a new course that was purported to be challenging and beautiful. He wrote back and said he might – but his son was also going to be with him. I got his son's e-mail and invited both.

On game day, I organized a car and driver. We were picked up at 7:30 a.m., drove an hour to the course, set up, and golfed, and also had a fabulous lunch. During the round, we talked about life, work, business, and just about everything except our potential deal. On the 18th fairway, he turned to me and said "Eli, I have decided to adopt your platform. I will ask my VP to work out the details, and we can get started on the first of the month."

I thanked him. That was all we said. Nothing else was discussed regarding business, but I won a long term deal that had monthly billing for three years.

### *Bethpage Black*

My home course, about five minutes away, is the world famous Bethpage Black. It was the host of the 2002 and 2009 US Opens, as well as many tournaments both regional and PGA. Playing it is a coveted life-time experience for any golf enthusiast.

There was a world-wide industry show in New York City, and I knew many of the Presidents and CEOs of the companies who were attending. Working with one of the tournament chairs, I invited 20 people to set aside an additional day at the conference to experience Bethpage in late October. On the day of the event, I sent a bus into New York City to collect them and all arrived about 11 a.m. for a warm up, lunch, and a round at this most famous destination.

I had sales interests with every participant. While some of these companies were on-going customers, I was propositioning others to take on my service. The day turned out to be one of those fall gems: temperatures in the low 60s, sunny, and just an amazing day.

Naturally, most of the golfers struggled and flailed around the course that day. After all, the world's best have shot high rounds there. As the day wore on, as the camera lady was running around from group to group, you could hear the laughter and joy of spending what turned out to be a whole day with industry peers in a visually perfect fall setting and a world famous venue.

I did not need to sell anything, and the effect of the success of the day was not lost on any whom attended. Yes, I continued to sell those existing clients, but I also opened seven new accounts as a direct result of this event, during the next 12 months.

In each follow-up meeting, there was always a reference to the memorable day at Bethpage Black.

Golf is a sport where a person is bound by honesty, decorum, and best behavior. The well-known sales truth, "people like to do business with people they like," fits perfectly into a business round of golf. This allows us, the sales persons, to demonstrate, through action, the kind of character we embody. It sends an important message to our future customers.

Hear a bonus interview with Eli at: sellingonthegreen.com/eli-goodrich.

"Correct one fault at a time. Concentrate on the one fault you want to overcome."

- Sam Snea

"A mediocre person tells. A good person explains. A superior person demonstrates. A great person inspires others to see for themselves."

- Harvey Mackay

# Creating Lifelong Friendships and Influential Networks through Golf

■ Cliff Theriault

I don't profess to be the world's greatest golfer, but I truly love the game. You can play for your entire life, at any level of competence. It is useful for recreation, competition, and networking. It's helped me expand my network and make lifelong friendships. These associations have, in turn, benefited many other lives. An unexpected bonus is that my business has also blossomed through the connections I've made.

When I was 10 years old, my parents moved us from the city of Chicago to the suburb of Glenview. Up to that point, I had very little contact with the game of golf. Our new home was four doors from the entrance to the public golf course, and my curiosity for the game was raised. While my father had played, he wasn't an avid golfer.

He had a set of clubs that I was able to use. Every evening, I would go to the course to chip and putt. It was September, and I didn't have member privileges or spare money to play. After 7 p.m., we would walk over and play three holes over and over until it got so dark that we couldn't see. I was hooked. The next spring, I heard of an opportunity to caddy at the local country club, and was quick to get training for the job.

I was the oldest of seven kids and, while we never went without anything we needed, there wasn't a lot of disposable cash to pay for the finer things. Caddying opened up a lot of doors for me. I had money to spend on clothes, bikes, sporting equipment, and, most importantly, my own golf clubs. I was able to open my own bank account and save money that eventually would pay for my first car.

Not only did I learn a lot about the game of golf, but I also learned a lot about life from the influential people that surrounded me. I became the regular caddy for a husband and wife who were the owners of a major sports franchise. They were very charitable, and were probably the most impressionable members that I became associated with.

Time went on, and I continued to play golf. I was fairly successful in my career, and fortunate enough to belong to a club, which led to playing in some charity tournaments. By this time, I was married with two young, healthy children. I felt it was time to give something back.

I became involved with the local chapter of the March of Dimes because it raised money to help combat a birth defect that I was born with and wound up on a golf committee for the annual tournament to raise money in the fight to reduce birth defects. Having played in other charity events, I had met a lot of local sports celebrities, and was able to get them involved in my quest.

These friendships led to involvement with other charity organizations. Two of my closest friends set up their own charities to help kids lead a more positive lifestyle, and to ensure that there were camps available for kids to attend, even if their parents didn't have the means to pay. During that time, I was coaching every sport that my kids were involved in, so I was able to parlay that friendship to get these two gentleman involved.

We set up football camps for professional players, mostly rookies, giving them opportunity to make money during the summer. We also set up a company to help kids obtain college scholarships. I can proudly say we helped a lot of kids.

We also played a lot of golf together, and my friends have both enjoyed successful second careers. Ron Rivera has gone on to become the head coach of the Carolina Panthers, after a successful career as an assistant coach with several teams- including my son's Little League team. Glen Kozlowski became a high school football coach, and has a radio show, Sports Central, on WGN Radio. We remain close, and I am very proud of their accomplishments.

Golf is a game anyone can play at any age. The PGA Tour has come up with the campaign of "Tee It Forward," to help golfers have more fun on the course and enhance their overall experience by playing from a set of tees best suited to their abilities. They also sponsor fundraisers that provide character building programs for youths, using golf to teach good values and decision making skills.

I am fortunate that my folks made that move to the suburbs in 1960. Many friendships and relations have been born out of golf. I have friends whom I have been playing with for over 35 years, and we hope to be playing until we can't take the club back anymore.

My life changed because I was introduced to the game of golf. People I caddied for helped shape my life. The relationships I formed through charity work helped influence my life. My family and I became closer as a result of their involvement in that charity work, and I am a better person today as a result.

This isn't "The Greatest Story Ever Told," but it's my story, and I am proud of it.

Cliff Theriault is the regional manager for CMG Financial, a privately held mortgage-banking firm headquartered in San Ramon, CA.

# There Are No Shortcuts to Building Relationships on the Green

■ Tami Belt

I grew up playing golf, before golf was cool, especially for girls. Years later, as golf gained popularity, the teasing subsided, and I realized the many valuable lessons learned from playing "the gentleman's game."

They call it "the gentleman's game" for a reason. The links on the local municipal golf course, where my dad was a PGA teaching pro, were lined with a cast of characters from CEOs and celebrities to construction workers and everything in between. Everyone followed course etiquette. In other words, players minded their manners and showed respect to fellow players.

Basic etiquette includes:

- Never walk on someone else's line
- Be quiet
- No distractions
- Don't leave the green until everyone has finished putting
- Tee off based on honors

Unlike other sports, you rarely hear about professional golfers being involved in scandals.

Here are a few of the lessons I learned on the links that apply to business:

- Play the ball where it lies. You have to deal with what is happening now.
- Sometimes you land in hazards. In business, there is no "get out of hazards free" card. You have to deal with sticky situations honestly and maneuver your way out. No matter how you landed in an undesirable position, how you respond is up to you.
- There are no mulligans. You only get one chance to make a first impression. You will have opportunities to make up for mistakes, but you must first deal with them.
- Every shot, good or bad, is worth the same. Whether something good happens or something bad, it is still just one thing. You can recover or capitalize on one thing at a time. No one shot or mistake defines you. It's how you recover that counts. Each stroke is one tiny part of an entire round.
- Bet on yourself. In golf, you have to pay to play. Pros pay an entry fee and bet on themselves to win. If they play well, they realize a return on their investment. If not, they don't get a trophy or a paycheck.
- Timing is everything. A good golf swing follows the line and tempo of a pendulum. If you try to power through it, you will disrupt the natural flow and fall short of your goal. There are no shortcuts. If you follow good form, the momentum will carry you through.
- Drive for show. Putt for dough. It's the little things that count the most. You can rush ahead at lightning speed, but if you fail to sink the deal you will never be ahead in the game.
- There is no such thing as a "gimme." You have to practice and master all aspects of the game. It's the little things, like customer service, quality control, and taking care of employees that win loyalty and customers.

"You can discover more about a person in an hour of play than in a year of conversation." — Plato

One of the best ways to get to know someone is to play a round. You will discover:
- Do they cheat?
- Do they have a temper?
- Are they polite?
- Are they a good sport?

A great way to build relationships is to play on a team in a charity golf tournament. No matter your level of expertise, everyone plays together and contributes value.

In business, there is no shortcut to building relationships, just as there is no shortcut to quality service or products. You can learn how to work smarter, but you never want to compromise on quality. When deciding whom you want on your team – employees, partners, customers, vendors – never compromise.

I served as a Big Sister with Big Brothers/Big Sisters for eight years and support the charity whenever I can. When I first launched my company, I was on a tight budget and couldn't afford to play in their annual charity golf tournament, so I volunteered to work the event.

I spent the day lounging on the green of the "Closest to the Pin" contest hole, soaking up sunshine and getting reacquainted with a colleague, Charli Carter, who used to work at a TV station.

We had never formally met prior to that day, but she knew my name from the Public Service Announcements I sent to her at the station. As we caught up, I discovered she was a personal friend of the Executive Director of Big Brothers/Big Sisters.

After the tournament, Charli introduced me to the Executive Director who appointed me to the Communications Committee of their Board and, later, contracted me to help the charity build relationships with donors. In addition, Charli invited me join the Task Force of Las Vegas Ride for Kids, a charity motorcycle ride that benefits the Pediatric Brain Tumor Foundation.

Her husband, Dave Carter, owns Carter Powersports and brought the ride to our city in 2004. He liked the work I did on the task force so much that he contracted my company to help his store with public relations. The relationship with the Carters and Las Vegas Ride for Kids continues. 2014 marks the 10th annual ride in Las Vegas.

You can tell the character of a man by how graciously he loses to a woman. As an example: One time I played in a charity golf tourna-

ment and won the Long Drive Contest. At the gathering, after the tournament, my friend, Bill, came over to congratulate me and said there was someone he wanted me to meet.

Bill was a sales executive at a local TV station which had been in the community for many years. We walked straight up to a well-known ad agency owner and Bill said with a smile, "Terry, I want you to meet the woman who out-drove you, today." I have to admit, I was a

little worried. The worry soon faded. Terry smiled, extended his hand and said, "It's a pleasure to meet you!"

Prior to the introduction at the golf tournament, we had never formally met, and only knew each other professionally. After that introduction, I received invites to a few of his events and even collaborated on a couple of projects.

The lessons I learned on the links have made a great difference in my business. They can for you as well.

Hear a bonus interview with Tami at: sellingonthegreen.com/tami-belt.

"A good golfer has the determination to win and the patience to wait for the breaks."

- Gary Player

"I always tried to turn every disaster into an opportunity."

- John D. Rockefeller

# A Fuzzy Golf Outing: How a Well Planned Event Can Make the Difference

■ Steven Wilson

Time on the golf course can be time well spent. It's all about how you approach the four to five hours you'll spend chasing a little white ball. You can work on your game or work on your career. Many men, and increasingly more women, are learning that a round of golf is most valuable when you share a cart with a current or future client.

As the Director of Special Events for "Golf Digest," part of my responsibilities was to run the corporate outing programs for the magazine's top advertisers. This featured some of America's top courses, where Fortune 100 companies would entertain guests. The hook was that my clients would pay a hefty fee so that a top golfer would share the day with their 60 or so guests.

Back when he was winning US Opens, Fuzzy Zoeller was a popular "talent" for high end corporate golf outings. And why not? He was amiable and knew how to play the corporate golf game. One time, at a famous club that regularly hosts a PGA TOUR event, Fuzzy was having a grand old time, sharing stories and jokes with each foursome that came to the Par 3 tee box that he played with all the guests. As it got later in the day, the jokes became longer, and that pushed our tight schedule a bit.

At around 4:30 p.m., I was on the tee box when I got a call on my walkie-talkie from the club's GM. He wanted to know why the group wasn't off the course yet and in the locker room, getting ready for cocktails and dinner. I understood the club had their schedule, but watching my client and their guests laughing hysterically at Fuzzy Zoeller's jokes was something that I just couldn't put a stop to.

It's a good thing I didn't. A few months later, I got a very nice letter from my client's Senior VP who was at the golf outing with Fuzzy Zoeller. He said that, although that day was the most expensive outing he had ever taken, it had the highest ROI of any one thing he had invested his company's money in that year.

This is not to suggest that you should get a top PGA TOUR player for your next outing. But rather, that you, too, can use a golf course to help you grow your business this season. It takes planning and a beautiful day, but when it all comes together, the results can be outstanding!

Hear a bonus interview with Steven at: sellingonthegreen.com/steven-wilson.

# Protocol and Politeness are Par for the Course

■ Dawn Bryan

"Eighteen holes of medal play will teach you more about your foe than will 18 years of dealing with him across a desk." - Grantland Rice, sportswriter

Social behavior (etiquette/manners) evolves differently within different cultures. Knowledge of certain sport traditions has come to represent a person's background, education, interests, and status.

Thus, whoever aspires to elevate or strengthen a business relationship through the game of golf needs to understand the rules, courtesies, and expectations that identify membership in this culture. Conversely, mistakes will surely result in lost sales and deal cancellations.

Played without the supervision of a referee or umpire, golf relies on the integrity of both players and spectators to conduct themselves appropriately. Golf culture is about respect for the others involved in the event, as well as an appreciation for the quality of the course itself. More complicated, confusing, and demanding than the novice player might assume, its rules—written and unwritten—go beyond the usual practices of sportsmanship.

Because the business round is about building and maintaining relationships, knowledge of golf etiquette can be more significant than skill, especially for the novice. And mastery of golf protocol is much easier and quicker than mastery of the game.

One of my clients—new to both corporate culture and golf—was appalled to learn that his (unintended) rude behavior on the course had registered not only with other members of his foursome, but had made a significant impression on the foursome behind, which happened to include his host's boss.

This was especially embarrassing, because he had been diligently preparing with both lessons and practice sessions.

Socializing in the clubhouse after the round, Clint's foursome was approached by a gentleman who greeted them heartily. His host then introduced Clint to the company CEO, who pointed his finger at Clint and roared—"So you are that guy in the blue shirt who was holding us up all day!"

Shocked, Clint did not know what to say. His host tried to rescue him by stating that Clint was a novice to the game, and asking his boss why they did not just "play through." The CEO laughingly said he figured that his VP of Operations was trying to develop his own interpersonal skills.

Needless to say, my client never heard from the company again, even though he did follow up on their business discussions and write a thank you note.

In retrospect, Clint recognized that, totally unaware of pace protocols, he had gone off to search for his ball (three times) rather than using a provisional ball, taken too long to make some shots, and stayed on the green after putting was over to record his score.

Not knowing the appropriate protocols and codes of social behavior kept him from "belonging" to the business-golf culture.

Whether you are invited to be a tournament spectator or an early morning player, basic rules and protocols apply. Remember, you are a guest.

The Considerate Spectator will:

- Dress appropriately. Wear sneakers or spikeless golf shoes. Dress comfortably for the weather, bringing hat, sunglasses, umbrella, and perhaps something to sit on.

- Become familiar with the list of prohibited items, which may include food and drink, lawn chairs, camera equipment, signs, and banners. Most tournaments, and some clubs, ban cell phones.

- Learn and follow the spectator rules and guidelines set down by the club and the association hosting the event and, if unsure, know to ask one of the volunteers for guidance.

- Always be quiet during play; keep movements to a minimum when players are about to swing; wait for all players to finish putting (putt out) before leaving the green area for the next tee.

- Understand how the game is played and scored. Medal play (stroke play) is a scoring system that involves counting the total number of strokes taken on each hole, during a given round or rounds

- Stay inside the ropes, and show respect for others by kneeling down so as not to block the views of others and by not moving in front of others who were waiting there first.

Spectators should not:

- Talk while someone is playing a stroke.

- Ask for autographs or photos during a player's rounds. Note: At some events these are permitted at certain times and places.

- Boo or heckle.

- Applaud a player's mistake.

- Wander/walk around a golf course while a tournament is being played.

The Knowledgeable Player will:

- Wear appropriate shoes and clothing for the course. Although basic clothing traditions prevail, club rules vary, some permitting a more casual approach. Generally, both men and women wear golf shoes with soft spikes, and women wear knee-length skirts, skorts, Bermuda shorts, or pants. Men wear slacks or long shorts and shirts with sleeves and collars.

- Ensure safety by not playing until players in front are out of range; not standing close to or directly behind the ball or hole when a player is about to play; alerting greens staff, nearby or ahead, when they are about to make a stroke that could endanger them; and shouting "fore" as a warning when there is immediate danger.

- Learn the terminology. Like most sports, golf has its own lexicon. Although words like "Par," "Bogey," and "Eagle" are common to even non-golfers, the novice may be baffled by "Albatross," mystified by "Bunker," and bewildered when asked to play in a Scotch Foursome.

- Strictly observe local notices, regulating the movement of golf carts and keep carts away from greens and hazards.

- Be ready to play as soon as it is your turn.

- Try to keep pace with the group ahead of you. Allow groups to "play through" when your pace is slowed.

- Understand the intricacies of golf etiquette, such as how many practice swings to take before a tee shot, who takes the pin, and rules for the tee box and putting green.

- Respect the rules and regulations of the course and treat caddies with respect and consideration.

- Always replace divots, repair ball marks and damage to putting green caused by golf shoes, and rake footprints from bunkers (sand traps).

- Let the winner of the previous hole tee off first, allow the player farthest from pin to hit first on each shot, and try to play at a reasonable pace. For the purposes of calculating handicaps, turn in every score in a timely manner.

- Know when to play a provisional ball.

In a new business situation, avoid offering bets, but accept them if offered by your client or boss. And most important: win with grace, and pay promptly if you lose.

In general, the host tips the caddie, but if you have a personal caddie, you may tip the caddie, even when you are a guest.

Players should not:
- Wear jeans, cut-offs, short shorts, or tank tops.
- Speak during another player's swing.
- Ask opponents what club they hit.
- Talk business if someone is facing a difficult shot or until the group members are settled into the game and are comfortable with one another
- Slow down other players.
- Stand in a place that causes your shadow to be cast across another player or that player's putting line.
- Walk through a player's putting line, as your footprints could affect the path of the putt.
- Continue play when lightning is in the area.

Golf etiquette is an important part of the business game. Your new cultural competence will put your host and the other players/spectators at ease, creating a context for developing new relationships, strengthening existing ones, and closing sales on the green or at the 19th Hole.

Hear a bonus interview with Dawn at: www.sellingonthegreen.com/dawn-bryant.

"Every day you miss playing or practicing is one day longer it takes to be good."

- Ben Hogan

"Trust is the glue of life. It's the most essential ingredient in effective communication. It's the foundational principle that holds all relationships."

- Stephen Covey

"I'm about five inches from being an outstanding golfer; that's the distance my left ear is from my right."

-Ben Crenshaw

"Golf is a game that is played on a five-inch course--the distance between your ears."

-Bobby Jones

# The Ability to Comeback

■ Dan Demuth

"The Comeback," is one of the most marveled parts of the sports world. It is an exciting thing to watch when the odds pile up against a team or individual, and they somehow find a way to overcome them. In light of Phil Mickelson's British Open comeback in 2013, let's break down some of the aspects of the comeback.

When our thoughts and actions stray from our goals, it creates some internal interference. Dealing with this interference is the key to getting back on track. The internal interference can manifest in a few different ways. These include:

- Focusing on what we don't want to do, rather than what we do want to do
- Allowing the past to control the future
- The need for perfection
- Negative perceptions clouding our judgment

No matter where the interference comes from, it takes practice and persistence to be able to realign yourself to focus on a comeback.

When we are not performing at our best, many of us get stuck and are unable to move forward. What we need to realize is that our perceived setback is actually an opportunity to comeback. Finding a way to let go of the interference happens through a change in your thinking.

You have the power to change your reality through a change in your thinking. It is important to keep an open mind with the ability to love ourselves in challenging times. If your thoughts are saying, "you can't do it," you won't be able to.

Anger towards oneself for making mistakes or underperforming stems from the fear of repeating those failed actions. You assume that you are going to keep making mistakes, which is why people sometimes simply give up as they accept failure. However, whether you have failed at something or are losing in a game, there is actually an opportunity. Letting go of the past makes room in your mind for the possibilities. This allows for movement in the direction of creating achieving your dreams. You have the power to create the future; forget about the past. Change your perception from "this is something I can't do" to "this is something I can do."

Phil Mickelson is an excellent example of the art of coming back. Mickelson has experienced many setbacks both on the course and in his personal life, dealing with the medical problems of his wife and mother, as well as his own issues.

The year of 2012 was a tough one for Mickelson, as his golf game seemed to be suffering. He even took time off, citing "mental fatigue." After winning countless tournaments, it was a surprise to see him struggling so much. Mickelson also dealt with a heartbreaking runner-up finish in the 2013 US Open on his 43rd birthday.

However, Mickelson was able to put all of this behind him going into the 2013 British Open. He played extremely well the week leading up to the tournament and used that as momentum to fuel his confidence. He spoke of his excitement, saying, "Coming out on top just gives me more confidence." He went on to play arguable his greatest back 9 ever, on the final day, to win his fifth professional title at the British Open, being the first person ever to win both the Scottish and British Opens in the same year. In an interview, after the game, Mickelson stated that he was playing some of the best golf of his career. He spoke of his approach, saying he remained focused on each shot. Playing as well as he ever had, Michelson never spoke of the ball as his target, only of his shots and the hole.

Mickelson also spoke of his love/hate relationship with the British Open, saying during the times of struggle, love was not what he felt. However, he did not let the setbacks from each hole affect him, while he continued to play the course.

He spoke of having a "minute-to-minute" relationship with the game, illustrating his ability to be in the moment while playing his game. To be able to achieve such amazing performances in his recent tournaments, Mickelson needed to be able to put his past mistakes behind him. His body language showed him focused and confident, only thinking about his current goals and targets, one shot and hole at a time. It became obvious that his game was an extension of himself.

Even though he has failed many times, Mickelson had no fear of failure. He turned his failures into opportunities to learn and improve on the next shots.

Although his golf game had gone through setbacks, he was still excited to keep playing and did not dread going into future tournaments. Mickelson is just another example of the powerful effect of the mindset. Keeping a clear mindset is important to allow ourselves to see the entire picture and not let our perceptions stray from reality.

Although Mickelson had not played his best in previous tournaments, he kept his mindset clear and knew that he was still an extremely talented golfer. The control of our own mindsets helps us to see, think, influence, behave, and perform in the direction of our goals, always returning strong from our setbacks.

Dan Demuth is president of Performance in Motion and author of the book: *Secrets of the Golf Whisperer: On & Off the Course*. You can learn more by visiting www.performanceinmotion.biz.

Hear a bonus interview with Dan at: www.sellingothegreen.com/dan-demuth.

# Why the Mental Game is Crucial to Both Golf and Business

■ Dr. Dan Schaeffer

Over the years, I've developed a variety of strategies to help people play golf better and get out of their own way. Consider that a golf swing takes about three seconds. If you shoot a 100, you only have to concentrate for a total of five minutes the entire round.

How well you play is determined by how well you control your mind game. So, the question is how do you control your mind game? I talk to many athletes about what they take onto a golf course that doesn't belong there--business problems or personal challenges. Can they just go out on the course, shut their mind down and play golf in their subconscious mind? I think they can. So, I give people some strategies to do that.

The question really is: Can anybody afford one second of distraction in anything they're doing — whether it's a business negotiation or a round of golf or a tennis match? So, one of the things that my athletes focus on is what distracts them.

The most distracting thing for professional football players, quarterbacks, hockey players, and other athletes is the way they talk to themselves. We have a method to identify what is distracting them before they go onto the golf course. That becomes critical in them being able to put their issues aside.

For example, if somebody goes out on the course, stands up over a tee shot and says to themselves, "I don't want to get this ball into the water," their subconscious mind, where the shot comes from, actually hears a negative command. What it hears is hit the ball in the water.

In terms of business, someone going into a business deal may mentally say, "I don't want to blow this business deal," "I don't want to give a poor presentation," "I don't want to screw up this testimony in court." This negative talk is the wrong mindset to be going in with and has a lot to do with controlling your mind game.

## *Using the Game of Golf for Growing Your Business*

Just recently, a company in Virginia wanted to get more copier and printer business from people. A bank sponsored me to do the program for them, and we had 200 CEOs, in two days, attend this event.

Why? It's because there was no pitch for copier and printer equipment and each person was allowed to invite whomever they wanted. In other words, they could bring their kid if he or she was a college golfer, or they could bring a prospect with them.

People have to be very careful about doing business on the golf course. If a guy comes out wanting to shoot his best game, and somebody is yapping about business, or somebody comes to the first tee discussing an order or sale, it's going to go south.

I've talked to professionals I've worked with in this program who've done exceptionally well, and they have said to me, "I use golf to determine the personality and the honesty of the person that I'm planning to deal it." They have also said, "I watch to see if a guy kicks a ball for a better lie; if so, I'm not doing business with him."

## *Using Golf to Build a Relationship with New Clients*

People hate to cold call. I have a whole process where people will profile a company and identify whom they need to talk to, who the decision-maker is. When they do that and find that the CEO of the company plays golf, they are home free.

I did this with a bank in Connecticut about three years ago. I wanted to talk the bank manager into doing a training program for them and this golf program. I called up the gatekeeper, Kathy, and asked her, "Can I speak to Jack?" And she said, "Well, he's busy. Send us an e-mail or send us some material."

I said, "Kathy, we have a problem." So, she said to me, "What's the problem?" I said, "Kathy, this is a golf call." So, she says, "Oh, you're one of those." I said, "Yes, I'm one of those." She said, "Well, let me see if he'll pick up the phone."

I said, "You want to have some fun?" She says, "Yeah." So, I asked, "Is there a golf ball around, anywhere?" She said, "On the next desk." I told her, "Go get the golf ball, hold the phone up, where he can see it, take the golf ball and point it toward the speaker of the phone and see how long it takes him to pick the phone up. Within seconds, he was picking up the phone."

I think business golf is about the relationship. If I was trying to sell you something and I took you out for a round of golf and then took you for a couple of drinks after the round was over, are you going to buy something for me?

It's a very interesting dynamic. The biggest challenge that businesses have today is how to get in front of potential clients and also those who can make a decision.

When I speak to companies about inviting their clients to one of my golf training programs, the response is sometimes "Well, they're probably not going to take the time to come to this."

My response is "No, they're not going to come to a weekend of dining out because they don't need to. They can go to dinner any place they want. They can go to the best steak house and be playing at Pebble Beach, tomorrow, with the help of their corporate jet; but they can't be guaranteed strokes off the golf game by doing that. You have to speak to their needs. What do executives really want? They want to improve their game, even if it means shaving a few strokes off."

What are some mental strategies golfers can use to improve their game if they want to use golf as a way to build business relationships?

If the competitive edge is to get in front of clients, and you want to get them to come to you, I would say the overall strategy would be to have a couple of really top golfers and send them out with the other good golfers.

I think if I was starting out, and I thought that the development of my business had to do with how well I played golf, I would take the necessary steps to improve.

Again, one of the most important things you can do is visualize. Where do you want to be? How do you want to be playing? What do you want your business to look like?

I can tell you all the mistakes people have made before they became my clients and the same goes for golfers.

People go out on a golf course, thinking about the last time they played this hole, and how bad it went. They don't use positive visualization. You want to know something? Jack Nicholas used visualization all the time. The big key is identifying distractions, shutting them down, and knowing how to do that.

How do you find out what distracts you, if you want to play better? I want people to listen to the way they talk to themselves, as they go and take their first lesson.

I think that a golf instructor should put mental strategies in their lessons because the game played between one's ears is one of the most important when it comes to golf.

Dr. Dan is president of Peak Performance Strategies LLC. You can learn more about Dr. Dan and his programs by visiting danschaeferphd.com and www.golfandthemindgame.com.

Hear a bonus interview with Dr. Dan at: sellingonthegreen.com/dan-shaefer.

"Don't look for excuses to lose. Look for excuses to win."

- Chi Chi Rodriguez

"Value the Relationship More than Making Your Quota."

- Jeffry Gitomer

# Get Your Free Bonus Audio

"Business Lessons from the Golf Course",
Just visit
SellingontheGreen.com/audio

# Glossary of Golf Terms

ACE – When a golfer makes a hole in one!

ADDRESS – The position of the golfer's body taken just before he or she hits the ball. "Addressing the ball" means the golfer is standing over the ball and preparing to hit the ball.

APPROACH – Your shot onto the green from the fairway.

APRON – The closely mowed area just around the edge of the green, often called the "fringe."

BACKSPIN – This is a reverse spin on the ball. It causes the ball to stop very quickly on the green.

BACKWING – The part of the swing that begins from the ground, going back over the top of the golfer's head.

BAIL OUT – This is a shot played to a safer part of the course. The bailout area is designed to serve as the target for weaker players when better players will be playing a riskier shot.

BALL MARKER – A coin or some other small token that is placed just behind the ball in order to mark the position of the ball on the green. This allows another player who is farther away to putt without hitting any of the balls that are closest to the hole.

BANANA BALL – A slang term for a slice. It curves in a banana-like shape.

BASEBALL GRIP – Holding a golf club like a baseball bat, where all ten fingers are on the club grip.

BEACH – A golf slang term for the bunker or sand trap.

BENT GRASS – Type of grass which is found in mostly northern climates. It is characterized by thin blades which grow densely and can be mowed extremely close, resulting in a felt-like smoothness to the putting surface.

BERMUDA GRASS – This is type of grass is found on courses in mostly southern climates. The grain of Bermuda grass greens can influence a putt, so golfers should be aware when they are putting with, against, or across the grain.

BIRDIE – Scoring 1 under Par for a hole. For example, scoring a 3 on a Par 4.

BITE – Backspin on the ball, stopping it very quickly on the green.

BOGEY – A score of 1 over Par on a hole. For example, scoring a 4 on a Par 3 hole.

BUNKER – Another term for a sand trap.

CADDIE – The person carrying a player's clubs during play. A caddie can offer assistance to the player in accordance with the rules.

CARRY – The distance that a ball must travel in the air before hitting the ground. If a player needs 100 yards to carry a water hazard, then they need to hit the ball in the air for 100 yards.

CASUAL WATER – Temporary puddles of rainwater on the course, due to rainfall. A player is not penalized for moving his ball out of casual water.

CHIP SHOT – An approach shot that is hit from close to the green (usually within a few yards of the putting surface).

CHIP IN – A chip shot into the hole.

CHOKE – Gripping lower than normal on the club ("choke down" on the club).

CHOP – Hitting the ball with a short, hacking motion.

CLUBHEAD – The part of the golf club attached to the end of the shaft; the hitting area of the golf club.

CLUBHOUSE – The area where players usually go to have refreshments after 18 holes.

COURSE RATING – This is the difficulty of a course. Usually, the higher the course rating the harder it is.

CUP – holds the flagstick in the hole.

DEUCE – A score of 2 on a hole!

DIMPLE – Small indentations on the golf ball.

DIVOT – A piece of ground that is taken up by the club, after hitting the ball. A good golfer ALWAYS replaces his divots and tamps them back down so they will grow back!

DOGLEG – A hole that is straight for a while then has a bend to the left or right.

DOUBLE BOGEY – A score of 2 over Par for one hole. These are not very good!

DOUBLE EAGLE – Describes a score of 3 under Par on any individual hole.

DOWNHILL LIE – The ball is on the down slope of a hill. When a right handed player addresses the ball his right foot will be higher than his left foot.

DRAIN – To sink a putt ("drain it").

DRAW SHOT – A controlled hook that goes from right to left (hit by a right handed golfer).

DRIVE – The tee shot.

DRIVER – Also known as the "1 wood," It's the club that hits the ball the farthest.

DROP – This is a way that you get the ball back in play after hitting a shot into the water or out of bounds. This also happens to waitresses when they carry too many plates.

DUB – A bad shot where the ball never leaves the ground; a "dubbed" shot.

DUFFER – can also be called a "hacker"; one who hits a lot of bad shots.

EAGLE – A score of 2 under Par on a hole. (e.g. a score of 3 on a Par 5 hole)

FACE – The area of the club head that makes contact with the ball.

FADE – This is a shot (for a right-handed golfer) that curves gradually from left to right.

FAIRWAY – This is the well-maintained area on the golf course that lies directly between the tee box and the green. The grass is cut really short here. You want to hit from this area if at all possible.

FAT SHOT – This is a shot which is not good. The club hits the ground behind the ball and results in a poorly struck shot that usually doesn't go very far.

FLUB – See dub above.

FOLLOW-THROUGH – The continuation of the golf swing to the end.

FORE – This is yelled when a player hits a shot toward another golfer. It's used to alert him/her of the oncoming ball.

FOURSOME – A group of four players.

FREE DROP – When you get to drop the ball and don't have to add a stroke to your score.

FRINGE – The closely cut area just around the edge of the green.

FRONT SIDE – The first 9 holes is usually referred to as the "front side."

GIMME – A putt so close to the cup that it will certainly be made. Others might say "it's a gimme" so the player doesn't have to putt it. He does however need to count this stroke to his score!

GRAIN – The direction that the individual blades of grass are growing on a golf course. The ball tends to roll faster with the grain and slower against it.

GREEN – Putting area on the golf course.

GRIP – The part of the shaft that is held by the golfer. This can also describe the way that a golfer is holding the club.

GROSS – Total number of strokes taken by the player on his round.

GROUNDING THE CLUB – Placing the club head on the ground behind the ball at address position.

HACKER – A golfer who is unskilled.

HANDICAP – The number of strokes a player may deduct from his actual score to adjust his score to that of a scratch golfer.

HAZARD – Any area to avoid like a sand trap, or body of water that will cause problems on the golf course.

HEEL – The part of the club head that is nearest to the shaft.

HOLE HIGH – Also known as "pin high'; An approach shot where the player's ball comes to rest even with the pin, but off to one side.

HOLE-IN-ONE – An Ace.

HOLE OUT – When a player completes the hole.

HONOR – The privilege of hitting first on the next tee. The "honor" is gained by having the lowest score on the preceding hole.

HOOK – To hit the ball and have it curve gradually from right to left (for right-handed golfers).

HOSEL – The hollow area of the club head that the shaft is fitted and secured to.

INTERLOCKING GRIP – A type of grip where the little finger of the lower hand is interlocked with the index finger of the upper hand.

IRON – A club with a metal head, which is not a wood!

JAIL – A golfer's term for a ball hit into a lot of trees which makes it very difficult to hit your ball out of…"in jail."

JUNGLE – A golfer's term for heavy rough or in the woods. (i.e. in the jungle).

KICK – A golfer's term for bounce. (I got a bad kick means I got a bad bounce)

LAG – To putt the ball with the intention of leaving it short of the hole so that the golfer is able to have a very easy putt on the next shot.

LATERAL HAZARD – Any hazard that runs parallel to the fairway.

LIE – The position the ball ends up when it comes to rest on the ground.

LINKS – Just another word for the golf course.

LIP – The top rim of the cup.

LOB SHOT – A shot that goes straight up in the air and then lands on the green, stopping quickly.

LOCAL RULES – Rules set by a particular golf course.

LOFT – A measurement, in degrees, of the angle at which the face of the club lies relative to a perfectly vertical face represented by the shaft.

MATCH PLAY – This is a form of competition by holes. Each hole is worth one point no matter how many strokes one player beats another by.

MEDAL PLAY – A form of competition decided by the overall number of strokes. This may also be referred to as stroke play.

MULLIGAN – An extra shot which is allowed if you hit a really bad first shot.

MUNICIPAL COURSE – Local public course.

NASSAU – A form of competition which breaks down the play into front 9, back 9 and overall 18 holes. A point is allowed for each nine and the total 18.

NINETEENTH HOLE – Another word to describe clubhouse. The restaurant and bar at the clubhouse that many players visit after 18 holes.

OFFSET – A club with the head slightly behind the shaft.

OUT-OF-BOUNDS – The area in which play is prohibited. If a

player's ball goes out of bounds, they must hit again from the same spot and take a penalty stroke.

OVERCLUBBING – Choosing a club that will hit the ball farther than needed.

PAR – The number of stokes that is recommended to take to finish a hole.

PENALTY STROKE – An additional stroke that is added to a golfer's score for a rules violation, going out of bounds, losing a ball, or various other situations.

PIN – The flagstick that is in the cup on the green.

PITCH – A short, high arcing shot that lands and stops quickly on the green.

PITCH AND RUN – Same as a pitch but hit with a lesser lofted club, which causes it to roll farther.

PIVOT – The rotation of the shoulders, waist, and pelvis during the golf swing.

PLAYING THROUGH – Allowing faster players to move ahead of the slower group.

PREFERRED LIE – A lie that may be improved by a player.

PRO SHOP – A golf course store that is operated by the golf pro.

PROVISIONAL BALL – Additional ball that is hit in if the first ball cannot be found. The player is then given a penalty stroke.

PULL – A ball that is hit to the left of the target (for right handers).

PUNCH THE GREENS – A punched green is a putting green that has been aerated.

PUSH – Also known as "push shot". A ball that is hit or pushed to the right of the target (for right handers).

PUTT – A shot hit with the putter on the green.

PUTTER – The club used to putt ball when on the green. It's often referred to as the "flat stick"

PUTTING GREEN – Area around the hole that is specially prepared for putting.

RANGE – This is the area for hitting practice shots.

READING THE GREEN – Determining which way the ball will curve on a putt based on the slope of the green.

ROUGH – Thicker grass area adjacent to the fairway.

ROUND – 18 holes of golf.

RUN – The distance the golf ball traveled after it landed on the ground.

SANDBAGGER – A golfer who tells others that he is a worse golfer than he really is. This is done to gain an edge in competition.

SAND TRAP – Areas on the golf course filled with sand that should be avoided.

SAND WEDGE – The iron that is used to hit the ball out of the sand bunker. It can also be used on short pitch shots.

SANDY – Getting out of a bunker and into the hole in two strokes.

SCRATCH GOLFER – A player with a handicap of 0. This player will normally shoot even Par or better every time.

SHORT GAME – The part of the game played close to the green. It includes pitching, chipping, and putting.

SHOTGUN START – A method of starting a tournament where all the golfers entered in that tournament begin play at the same time.

SIDE – This is a term, used to refer to the front and back 9s. Front "side" means the front 9 holes and back "side" is the back 9 holes.

SIDEHILL LIE – This is a lie when the golf ball is resting on a slope.

SLICE – This is a shot struck by a right handed golfer that curves severely from left to right.

SLOPE RATING – USGA term for the difficulty of a course for Bogey golfers relative to the USGA Course Rating (which represents the difficulty for scratch golfers). The higher the slope, the more difficult the course plays for Bogey golfers. Slope ratings range from 55 to 155. A slope rating of 113 is considered average.

SNAKE – A putting game where whoever three-putts first, gets a "snake" and keeps it until someone else three-putts. Whoever has the snake at the end of the round will usually treat the other players to a beverage.

STARTER – A person responsible for sending the groups of players off the first tee. The starter is normally located somewhere close to the first hole.

STIMPMETER – A device used to calibrate the speed of the greens by applying a known force to a ball and measuring the distance traveled in feet. A reading between 5 and 11 is the normal range with 5 being slow and 11 being very fast!

STROKE – This is the number of shots or additional swings you are given to even out the match. It's also the term used for swinging a golf club at a golf ball and hitting it.

SUDDEN DEATH – Breaking a tied match by playing extra holes. The first player to win a hole is the winner.

SUMMER RULES – Normal rules on the course, according to the rulebook.

SWEET SPOT – The center point on the face of the club; the ideal location on the club to hit the ball.

TAKEAWAY – This is what a golfer does when he starts the backswing.

TEE – Used to hold the ball up for driving. Also the term for the area where play begins on a particular hole.

TEXAS WEDGE – A term given for the putter when it is used from off the green. When a player's ball stops short of the green, the putter might be a better choice over the wedge due to the firmness of the ground.

THREESOME – A group of three players. A single player playing his own ball competes against two others.

TIGHT FAIRWAY – Narrow fairway with very little area on either side to miss.

TOE – This refers to the part of the club farthest from where it joins the shaft.

TRAJECTORY – The flight path of the ball. If it goes way up in the air it is referred to a high trajectory.

TURN – When you finish the first 9 holes and are "turning" to start the back 9 holes.

UNPLAYABLE LIE – A particular lie from which the ball cannot be hit. For example, if it's up against a tree or rock and the player cannot hit it.

WAGGLE – The small movement of the club head, back-and-forth, just prior to the player taking a swing.

WEDGE – An iron used for short shots that need a high trajectory.

WHIFF – To swing and miss the golf ball.

WINTER RULES – Local golf rules that permit the player to improve the lie of the ball in the fairway without a penalty.

WOOD – A club which is used for shots requiring a lot of distance.

WORMBURNER – The term for a shot that skims very low along the ground.

Made in the USA
Lexington, KY
23 July 2017